When a Lie Becomes the Truth

Jackie Harden

Jackie Harden
Newark, New Jersey

Cover Design: Ravi Lynn
Editing: Robin Devonish and Maria Romero
Interior Layout: Joy E. Turner - JetSet Communications & Consulting

ISBN 13: 978-0-692-71461-4
ISBN 10: 0692714618

www.jackieharden.net

Printed in the United States of America

Dedication

For Maxine, Marty, Scott, Joel, Kristen and the babies I conceived but did not birth. Your life does matter!

I also dedicate this book to my Mom, Nannie Mae -- my buddy, chum, and pal! Your legacy of love, hard work, laughter, strength, and courage will live on forever.

No more LIES!

*****   *****   *****   *****

Prelude

I had hoped that my mother – Maxine - would have had the conversation with "Mom" – Miss Nan, my grandmother, who we call "Mom" - that was so important to me. Yes, it's a conversation about the past, but the failure to face the truth and to have this conversation has profoundly affected my family.

What was tremendously important for me to know about my identity was totally dismissed by my elders. Not only was it dismissed, but a lie was concocted to cover up inappropriate behavior that resulted in children being born into a false reality. The refusal to tell the truth created a wound that became deeper over time. As with any wound that is not properly treated, it becomes infected, creating germs that fester and ooze with bloody pus, which is exactly what happened within my family. The lie was like a dark cloud that followed me everywhere I went and a mask that I was forced to wear.

As I tell the story, I have chosen not to take sides. Instead, I seek to understand more deeply what motivated the actions of my mother – Maxine - and my grandmother – Miss Nan - "Mom." I have come to the realization that had it not been for my grandmother taking my brother to raise him as her own, I may never have known him. Although "Mom" never acknowledged the truth regarding the dynamics of our family, she made sure that we knew our extended family, and that they knew us. "Mom" truly loved her family -- it is evident by all that she did for us.

Miss Nan, my grandmother - "Mom" - always cheered for the underdog. I believe it was the result of considering herself an underdog. In her last days, just before her death, she talked about being ostracized by family and friends for having a child out of wedlock. She talked about how hard it was for a single mother back in 1940. She talked about how black folks ridiculed her for being fair-skinned and white folks discriminated against her because she was black. She would often say, "I was too light for black folks and too dark for white folks!" But she worked hard and always took care of her family. The irony of this story centers around Miss Nan, my "Mom"; although she was a loving grandmother, she had a dark side, which is where she hid the pain and kept secrets. Was my "Mom" a co-conspirator in a major cover-up? Or did she believe that she had no choice but to enforce the lies? As you read on, you will decide for yourself. Whatever your answer, it is clear that my "Mom" was a key agent in creating a web of deception, which is the essence of this book.

I share this story not to place blame but to expose the truth about a complicated family story. It's a tangled web, but at its core, I believe this is a love story. My "Mom" loved us -- her grandchildren -- as her biological children so deeply that she sacrificed her entire life for us. We were her life! Everything she did was for us, about us, and with us... I am because you were "MOM"... Thank you!

Acknowledgements

First and foremost, I thank the Creator of the Universe for giving me the strength to not only survive but blossom and to find my voice. I also thank the powerful women in my family who were there for me during the tough times. These women taught me by example what it means to love and to persevere.

A special thank you goes out to my brothers. The older I get, the more I value our relationship. Thank you for always keeping it real with me and for allowing me to be who I am with you (and for loving me still).

Jasmine Victoria, you are "the star of my story" and I am so proud to call you my daughter and my friend. I thank God for you, for many reasons, but especially because you gave me a reason to live. You gave me a reason to seek the truth and to tell the truth. You gave me a reason to clean up my act. And in being honest, I was able to face the truth myself and came to realize that what was making me feel crazy inside, wasn't my fault. Through loving and caring for you, I learned the power of unconditional love. Every sacrifice I made to provide for you and to help you protect yourself was worth it. Finally, I thank you for encouraging me to tell my story.

Contents

Introduction   9

Chapter 1   The Memorial Service   13

Chapter 2   The Lie   25

Chapter 3   Daddy's Little Girl   31

Chapter 4   The Move to Newark   51

Chapter 5   Terminating Life   69

Chapter 6   "Olan" - "O": Orlando L. Covington   77

Chapter 7   Welcome to Motherhood   85

Chapter 8   Joel and Me   97

Chapter 9   Addiction and Recovery   115

Chapter 10   The Groton Experience   139

Chapter 11   How a Lie Became the Truth   153

Chapter 12   Reflection   163

Chapter 13   The Grapevine   175

Chapter 14   Truth   181

About the Author   190

> "The simple step of a courageous individual
> is not to take part in the lie. One word of
> truth outweighs the world."
>
> ~ **Aleksandr Solzhenitsyn**

INTRODUCTION

This book is about my life. It's my truth about my childhood; of what I witnessed and experienced that greatly affected the woman I've become. There was an unspoken agreement in my family that I would keep secret what went on behind closed doors. The events of my childhood were so chaotic and crazy that it almost took my lifetime to sort them out – to make sense of the unthinkable.

My hope is that as I expose my truth, you, the reader, will get in touch with yours. Quite frankly, I am tired of pretending to be someone I am not. I am tired of keeping secrets for other people. I am tired of denying within my spirit that I was hurt, abused, not protected, not truly loved, and not valued.

My story is not fatalistic because somehow by the grace of God I came to realize that my childhood experiences were not my fault. I happened to be born into a set of circumstances beyond my control. The parents I thought would love and protect me simply did not. Yes, I had a roof over my head, food to eat, and clothes to wear, but, since the core of my identity was based on a lie, everything about my life seemed to be one huge lie.

I have wanted to tell my story for a very long time, but keeping this secret nearly cost me my life: I was suicidal, depressed and felt isolated. When I gave birth to my one and only child, I was determined to end the cycle of lies. I desperately wanted my daughter, Jasmine, to have an opportunity to experience the fullness of life. I remember asking God to help me be a good mother. Realizing that I was merely the vessel God used to bring this new life into the world, I believed that if I asked God to use me for His

Glory, He would. It was from that point that I began to tell the truth. As I spoke the truth, as painful as it was to recount, it was liberating. Initially, I was angry – angry about the lies, the deception and the lack of protection. But as I shared my truth with Jasmine, I saw how it empowered her, which helped me to begin healing. So, I have decided to share my truth with you. I'm an ordinary woman who has faced some extraordinary circumstances. And, what almost killed me, made me stronger. There were many times when I didn't think I could make it through, but somehow deep within me was a voice encouraging me to hold on and when I would look into Jasmine's eyes I always saw hope. Jasmine's life depended on my life.

There are several pivotal moments along the way, which I will share. Some of the decisions I made I believe were the result of divine intervention. Hence, I remain eternally grateful for Universal Power; that all-knowing spirit that pushed me to make good decisions.

I have let go of the baggage that had become my bondage. Somehow, I think you *know* my story – there's a universal connection among us all. My story is yours and vice versa. There's a spiritual "knowing". Life can be painful, but there's a side of life that's joyful, where peace resides. That's where I want to be. That's where I want us to meet!

I'm tired of sending my representative into the world. The name I have used for the past 40 years isn't my name; it's the name I was forced to use as part of the web of lies spun around me. I became Jacquie Chavez – someone I was not, and that name became part of the persona I used to interact with the world. Even though I grew to like Jacquie Chavez, that's not who I am. The

11

name I was given at birth is Jacquelin Victoria Hurtman (nicknamed Jackie), and I'm ready to share her story. I have connected with her thoughts, her feelings, her desires, her pain and disappointments to proclaim her victory. Here's my truth!

> "In a room where people unanimously
> maintain a conspiracy of silence,
> one word of truth sounds like a pistol shot."
>
> **~ Czesaw Miosz**

CHAPTER 1

The Memorial Service

Just before John Hurtman died, I went to visit him in the hospital with my brothers Joel and Jon Scott (who we call by his middle name, Scott). John Hurtman had a heart attack and a mild stroke. He was hooked up to all kinds of tubes and could hardly speak, but he was aware of his surroundings and knew we were present. He recognized us and called each of us by name. I will always remember that he referred to Jon Scott as a "champion." During our visit, we reminisced about childhood experiences. It felt a bit awkward to me because there was information that my brothers and I wanted from him. John was our father; however, he only accepted Joel as his biological child. There was a web of deception surrounding him and the women he had children with, our biological mothers.

We had questions that we didn't dare ask. Not at this moment when his health was failing. So we stood around trying to make light of the situation. Before we left the hospital room, somehow we ended up stacking our hands on top of his. Dad's hands were laid on his stomach just below his chest. Joel placed his hand on Dad's, I placed my hand on Joel's, and Jon Scott slammed his hand down on mine. A few weeks later, John Hurtman died.

On July 2, 2003, Joel called to inform me of our Dad's death. I wanted to be a part of the memorial service. My brothers didn't want to participate, but I certainly did. I wasn't going to let my father's wife at the time of his death, Joanne, bury my Dad without having "my moment of truth". I believe Joel pressured Joanne into contacting me and she asked me to read a scripture she'd selected. I agreed, but I told my brothers that I was going to tell the truth - our truth - when I got up to speak.

The memorial service was held at Saint Aidan's Episcopal Church, a small church located in Cheltenham, Pennsylvania. The church was filled with a few family members, lots of my father's friends, his wife Joanne's immediate family, and folks from the community. A few of my brother Joel's friends were also there. I sat in the second row directly behind Joanne. My brothers Joel and Jon Scott sat in the rear of the church.

When I got up to read the scripture, I was very calm and poised outwardly, but inside I was extremely nervous. Here it was, my chance to set the record straight. After I had read the scripture Joanne selected for me to read (John 14:1-6), I called out for my brothers to come forward to stand with me at the podium in front of the congregation. I waited for them to take their position, one on each side of me but slightly behind me. I announced, "These are my brothers Jon and Joel and John Hurtman is our father."

Since my father had woven a tight web of deception and sold the world a lie about who he was and how his children came to be, I stood before God and Satan hoping that my testimony would secure John's permanency in Hades. The church was so quiet – as the saying goes "you could hear a rat piss on cotton!" I had everyone's attention. From the corner of my eye, I could see Joanne lower her head.

I went on to explain to all those gathered that John Hurtman married Miss Nan many years ago. Nan's daughter, Maxine, is mine and Jon Scott's mother. My father divorced Nan and later married a woman called Martha "Marty" Newsome. I stated that Marty isn't here today, but she raised Scott and me and she is Joel's mother. I went on further and said that during my Dad's marriage to Marty, Joanne appeared on the scene and engaged in an adulterous relationship with my father for many years. When Marty and Dad were finally divorced, he married Joanne. "That's who John Hurtman really was, and I just want you to know that we are his children."

I looked at Jon and asked him if he wanted to say something. He stepped forward to the microphone and said "Thank you for attending this funeral service for our father. Yes, I'm the oldest of John's kids and everything my sister Jackie just said is true." I then looked at Joel and said, "Do you want to say anything?" He said "No."

Needless to say, after that, the mood in the church changed. I could feel the shift. It was as if everybody was holding their breath and all the oxygen had been sucked out of the room. What just happened?

The minister came forward and delivered a brief eulogy. He read what had been typewritten on the program. Then he asked if anyone wanted to come forward to say anything about John Hurtman. He asked that the remarks be brief. I remember a middle-aged brown-skinned African-American woman that came forward to say a few kind words about him. Then one of Joanne's relatives came forward. I believe it was Joanne's niece; she was a young white woman. She looked to be in her mid-twenties. She had tattoos on her arms and a stud earring in her nose. She said a few kind words and took her seat. Then my brother Joel came forward. Joel said, "As bad as my father was, he had some redeeming qualities." He went on to talk about Dad's business acumen and how it was Dad who taught him to be the businessman he'd grown to be. Joel talked about how our Dad was a superior chess player and had taught many others to play the game. Joel thanked everyone for coming and took his seat.

My father's widow Joanne didn't say a word. She was probably in a state of shock. Yes, I said it! I spoke the truth; I exposed her, and I did it publicly! My inner voice screamed, and it dared Joanne to try to refute what I said. At the conclusion of the service, the minister announced that the repast would take place in the basement of the church. I saw Joanne stand up and make her exit heading to the room where the refreshments were to be served. I turned around to acknowledge members of my family: my Aunt Rosalie and her daughters, cousins Valerie, Gail, and Doris. We walked toward the rear of the church, made our exit to the church lawn and met up with Jon and Joel. A few people came up to us to express their sympathy as well as their shock over what they just witnessed. I wish the memorial service for my Dad had been tape recorded because I really want to hold those moments forever in my mind.

That was the first time I publicly shared my identity as well as my brothers. I am proud of that moment. Sure, I could have acted like my father was a great man. I could have stood before the congregation and shared pleasantries. I could have told a story that would have made him sound like a loving husband and a pillar of the community. But why would I do that? This is the man who didn't even admit that he was my biological father.

Maxine, Mom, and John

My grandmother, Nannie Mae Phipps, Miss Nan, who we refer to as "Mom", was born in rural Newton, Georgia in 1922 to Candace Victoria Washington and Joseph Phipps. She had three sisters and three brothers. The second to the last child, she was the youngest girl in her family and had one younger brother. Her mother and father owned the farmland where they lived. They raised cows, chickens, turkeys and some seasonal crops. My great-grandmother Candace, "Granny", was self-taught; she could read and write which was very rare for a black woman of that time. Given her ability to read, she was well respected by both the white and black communities. "Granny's" mother was white, and her father was of Jamaican heritage. There was also Cherokee Native American blood running through her veins. Joseph Phipps was also of mixed heritage, so my grandmother and her siblings were all fair skinned with "good hair." "Granny" insisted that her children attend school, which meant that everybody had to get up before dawn to milk the cows and do their chores before attending school. The walk to school was approximately five miles each way. All of the children graduated high school, except for my grandmother. Granny was sick a lot so my grandmother, Miss Nan, was the one who took on the responsibility of caring for her. My grandmother was only able to complete the ninth grade because by that time Granny needed full-time attention. Also, there was plenty of work on the farm that needed to be done.

When my grandmother was 18, a young dark-skinned man started coming by to see her. One afternoon during a visit, they had intercourse, resulting in pregnancy. My grandmother gave birth to a baby girl (Eleanor Maxine). There is no last name on Maxine's birth certificate. As an unwed mother, my grandmother became the scourge of her family. Her father, Joseph Phipps, didn't acknowledge Maxine, and her mother "Granny" encouraged her to give the baby away. Miss Nan refused to give her baby girl away.

When Maxine was eight months old, her Aunt Rosetta (Granny's sister) took Maxine to East Orange, New Jersey to live with her. Soon after that, maybe a year later, my grandmother Miss Nan went to New Jersey and while there she filled out an application at Thomas A. Edison, a major manufacturer of war equipment at that time. When she received a phone call notifying her that she was hired, she moved in with Aunt Rosetta.

My grandmother caught the bus to and from work, so did a man named John Hurtman. My grandmother must have been 22 years old at this time, and John was two years her senior. My grandmother, Miss Nan, had fair skin, long curly hair, and a shapely body. She wasn't well-educated, though – she only completed the ninth grade. John Hurtman, on the other hand, was a well-educated man, who spoke with authority and had full command of the English language. John Hurtman had a slender build and stood six feet two inches tall with a medium brown complexion. He was left-handed, however, when he was 22, his left hand was cut off by a machine he was cleaning. He never told me the story of exactly how he lost his arm, but he did tell me that he had to learn to write with his right hand. He wore a prosthetic arm most of the time. He would strap the arm on before putting on his clothes. He could do just about everything with one arm.

While riding the bus to work one day, he struck up a conversation with my grandmother Nan. Soon after, it became routine for John and Nan to sit together on the bus and talk. Eight months later they were married. Nan said that what really made her decide to marry John was the fact that he was good with Maxine. Back then, in the 1940s, it was taboo to have a child out of wedlock. The fact that John accepted her and her baby Maxine seemed absolutely wonderful to my grandmother. Even though I never saw any wedding pictures, I was told that they were married in Aunt Rosetta's house.

John had the gift of gab, as they say. He could talk to anyone; he was quite charming in a sly kind of way. John Hurtman was a salesman and a wannabe entrepreneur. He wore a suit and necktie every day without exception. Wing-tipped shoes finished off his signature look. He was born and raised in Newark, New Jersey. He attended Barringer High School and graduated with honors.

Maxine was a beautiful chubby toddler with a golden brown complexion and thick long curly hair. She was the spittin' image of her mother Nan, only darker brown. No one ever mentioned who Maxine's biological father was, but he lived in Newton, Georgia because that's where Nan lived when Maxine was born. Maxine grew up thinking that John was her father. John was the only father she ever knew.

Miss Nan grew to be crazy about John. He was handsome, intelligent, and a lot of fun. Most importantly, he accepted her baby girl and treated her as if she were his own. Nan and John wanted more children. In fact, Nan conceived twice – both times she miscarried. She never spoke a word about the loss of her two babies until much later in life.

John and Nan used to play cards, gamble among family and friends, and drink liquor. They were a handsome couple, well respected in the community and by appearances one would think that life was grand for them. They moved from East Orange to Trenton, New Jersey with John's mother and then moved to a quaint house in a nice neighborhood in Reading, Pennsylvania. John Hurtman required a lot of attention, so Nan focused mostly on him. John was truly the king of his castle. As such, he called the shots and maintained absolute control.

Nan kept her daughter Maxine dressed up in beautiful dresses and patent leather shoes. From the outside looking in, it appeared that all was well. But, Maxine was becoming defiant which was expressed by the way she refused to keep her room clean and neglected to do other household chores. She wouldn't follow her mother Nan's instructions, which resulted in Maxine getting whooped; Nan didn't hesitate to beat Maxine. But, the beatings only made Maxine more defiant. As previously stated, John had absolute control. He came and went at will, using his sales expeditions as an excuse to be away from home. When he was at home, he focused a great deal of attention on Maxine. Nan didn't think much of it. John really enjoyed playing games with Maxine, and Maxine really liked getting his attention.

Over time, the game changed and before long John was touching Maxine inappropriately. If Nan had paid attention, she would have seen the situation and the sadness in Maxine, but she either refused to see it or was simply unable to bring herself to see because then she would have had to take some responsibility to protect her daughter. Instead, Nan ignored the signs. What may have appeared as subtle, possibly normal jealousy between mother and blossoming daughter developed into resentment and was further masked by Nan as discipline. Could the mother be jealous of her daughter?

Nan and Maxine circa 1951.

When Maxine tried to tell her mother what Daddy was doing to her, Nan refused to believe her. She called Maxine a liar. Nan grew cold and spoke harshly of and toward her daughter. She was demeaning and rude toward Maxine. As a result, Maxine became more defiant, angry and withdrawn. Nan beat her both physically and emotionally while John continued to abuse her sexually. She – Nan - told Maxine that she would never amount anything – she said: "You're nothing, and you'll never be nothing!"

Nan and John Hurtman

> "The cruelest lies are often told in silence."
>
> ~ *Robert Louis Stevenson, Virginibus Puerisque*

CHAPTER 2

The Lie

Most men of his generation wanted a son and John was no exception. Unfortunately, his wife Nan had been unable to carry a baby full-term. Somehow, at some point, John must have decided that Maxine would have his baby because soon after Maxine graduated from high school, she became pregnant. Maxine had put on quite a bit of weight during her teen years, so during the first few months of her pregnancy, it wasn't noticeable to most people. To keep the secret about her pregnancy, when Maxine was six or seven months pregnant, John arranged for her to stay in a rooming house in Philadelphia. John and Nan would visit her on weekends when they could. For the most part, Maxine was left alone, in total isolation. She stayed in the attic. Her life was being controlled by the dictates of Nan and the abuse of John.

As fate would have it, Maxine gave birth to a male child. That's just what John and Nan wanted. The baby was born at the University Of Pennsylvania Hospital on January 31, 1960; she named him Jon Scott Hurtman. The name of the child's father was not provided on the birth certificate. Nan took the baby as soon as he was born. She declared that she would raise the baby as her own. Evidently, Maxine was sworn to secrecy about the entire experience. Nan and John told everybody that they had adopted the baby. Maxine had to act like the baby was her brother - an adopted brother. Nan adored "her" new baby boy. She forcibly took over the care of "Scottie", as the family lovingly called him. Nan was elated to finally have a son. At last, she had the baby boy that she couldn't deliver to her husband herself.

After the baby was born, Maxine returned to Reading. John, Nan, Maxine, and Scott all lived under the same roof in a small house in Reading, Pennsylvania. John continued to have sex with Maxine even after Scott was born. But Nan acted like she was unaware of what was going on between her husband and her daughter Maxine. Family members who lived nearby were a little suspicious of the situation and started to question Nan about her baby boy, but she adamantly stuck by her story of the adoption and tried to sound convincing. And Maxine just went along with it.

Outside the home, Nan worked hard as a seamstress. She was self-taught with superb skills, and could make anything. She quickly moved up through the ranks and became the first black supervisor at the sewing factory near her home in Reading. She liked to tell the story of how she worked at a unionized shop and when she became supervisor some of the white women walked out, but the owner of the business said that those other women could be replaced, but Nan was too valuable to lose. Nan was gifted; she could look at stitching and know if it was off by an eighth of an inch, plus she was quick. In the sewing industry, money is earned by the piece (or garment); my grandmother was fast and accurate.

Maxine was 19 years old when she gave birth to her first child, Jon Scott. She didn't talk about the pregnancy or the birth; this was kept strictly secret. No one in the family other than John, Nan and Maxine knew the truth about Maxine's son, Scott. By age 21 Maxine was pregnant again. The second pregnancy was NOT kept secret, and Maxine was not sent away. This time, Maxine came up with a tale; she said that she was impregnated by a young man named Joe Queen. Soon after the baby was born, John Hurtman reported this "Joe Queen" to the authorities and falsely accused him of not providing financial support to Maxine. The story was contrived that Joe Queen went to jail for non-payment of child support.

The second child was born at Reading Hospital on April 12, 1963. The child was named Jacquelin Victoria Hurtman – that's me. When Maxine went into labor, I don't know if anyone went to the hospital with her. I was never given any information about my birth. The only name printed on my birth certificate is mine and the name of my mother Maxine Hurtman -- no father was named.

I was affectionately referred to as "Jackie" by family and friends. Since Nan didn't like girls -- at least that's what she frequently told Maxine -- the responsibility of raising me fell on Maxine. When I was four months old, Maxine moved into her own apartment, which was located a few blocks from her mother's house.

By this time, John had begun staying away more often. It wasn't long after I was born that John moved to Philadelphia to be with a white woman by the name of Martha "Marty" Newsome. John had met her during a political campaign in Reading. It's difficult for me to imagine how he ever got close to Marty, but he did. John took my brother to Philadelphia to meet Marty, and eventually, he took Jon to live with Marty in the small apartment she had rented in the Germantown section of Philadelphia.

I have always wondered: what makes a man do what John Hurtman did? Why didn't Nan stop it or, at least, intervene at some point? Why didn't Maxine fight back, run away, or tell somebody? These are questions I have wanted answers to my entire life!

Nan with the women from the sewing factory.

> "Truth without love is brutality, and love without truth is hypocrisy."
>
> **~Warren W. Wiersbe**

CHAPTER 3

Daddy's Little Girl

My father was 44 years old when I was born; my mother Maxine was 22. My first memories of my Dad begin on a fateful day when he came back to Reading, Pennsylvania to ask me if I wanted to live with him in Philadelphia or stay in Reading with Maxine. I was only 2½ years old, but I remember that moment like it happened yesterday. I really wanted to be with my father, so I left. I don't remember how we got to Philadelphia. I think we drove.

I have pleasant memories of those early days in Philadelphia. Marty, by then my father's fiancée, bathed and dressed me, but it was my Dad who took me everywhere with him. Before I started school, we spent a lot of time together. Since Scottie was three years older than I, he was already enrolled in school.

I remember going to the park with my father to feed the squirrels and pigeons. I remember going to one of his favorite local restaurants called the Toddle House to have breakfast with him; he liked his eggs sunny-side up. No one was a stranger to my Dad; he would talk to anybody -- John Hurtman really liked to talk. I remember there was a handicapped white guy named Bud who was wheelchair-bound; he had cerebral palsy. His speech was slurred, and he would sit at the corner of Chelten Avenue and one of the major crossroads. He had a steel cup, and people would drop money in his cup as they passed by. Not only did my father drop coins in this man's cup, but he made it a point to engage in conversation with him. That always stayed with me.

Soon after I was taken by my father to Philadelphia, we moved into a spacious house located at 403 West Abbottsford Avenue. It was a single family home in the

Germantown section of Philadelphia. We lived directly across the street from a beautiful park. I was in awe of this huge, luxurious house and remember it distinctly. The front lawn of the house was on an incline covered with ivy. There were two sets of steps leading to the front door. As soon as you entered the front door there was a foyer with a curved slated floor; the space was approximately 30 feet by 10 feet. The distance from the front door to the door leading to the living room was approximately 15 feet. There was a wood-burning fireplace in the living room; straight ahead was a full dining room area with an oak dining room table and a matching china cabinet. The kitchen was rather small, only large enough for a stove, a counter used for food preparation with cabinets underneath, a double-sink, and, of course, a refrigerator. There was a staircase that led from the kitchen to the second floor, leading to the small office behind the master bedroom. The master bedroom was huge; Marty put two full-sized beds together for my father and her to sleep on. When we moved into the house, I didn't want to sleep in my bed so on many occasions I slept between Dad and Marty.

There was a full dresser and mirror against the wall of the master bedroom near the door that led to the hallway. On one side of the bedroom was the doorway that led to the piano room. When you entered the piano room from the master bedroom, a Steinway piano was on the right. Marty created a study area on the left side of the room for Scott and me to do homework each night. The door on the opposite side of the master bedroom led to the hallway. The bathroom was at the end of the hallway on the left, and the stairway leading to the living room was across from the bathroom.

My room was across the hall from the bathroom. Coming up the steps from the living room you had to make a sharp right turn to enter my room. I had a high-post mahogany bed, with a small stepladder to climb into bed. My dresser was a huge mahogany piece of furniture with lots of drawers. Marty gave me a hand-made dollhouse with hand-made miniature furniture. The dollhouse sat on a large windowsill near the doorway leading to Scott's room. In order to get to my brother Scott's room, you had to walk through my room around my bed. There was a door that led to the flight of stairs leading to Scott's room, which was in the attic. It was a large room. He had two twin-sized beds, a chest of drawers and a table. He had a medium-sized tank where he kept reptiles, and for a while, he had a snake (not sure what kind it was). There was a huge closet in his room which is where we stored our games and toys. We even had a full basement that Marty used as the laundry room. She always hung our clothes on a line to dry. The garage door was accessible from the basement. Marty truly set us up nicely. My father struck gold with her. Marty was everything that Nan wasn't: young, white, rich and educated.

My Dad was a strict disciplinarian who expected his children to speak properly and act appropriately at all times. He expected me to listen to him and learn. Therefore, I paid very close attention to him. He told me he loved me on a regular basis. He used to ask me if I knew how much he loved me. I would ask, "Daddy, how much do you love me?" He would answer, "A bushel and a peck!" Whenever I didn't feel well, he would give me special attention. For some reason I always had problems with my stomach; I got stomach aches quite a bit, and my father would rub my stomach to try to ease the pain. At age three, I had my appendix removed.

John Hurtman with Jackie and Scottie.

My father had a very strong stern voice. He was articulate and deliberate when he spoke. He exuded confidence and always took control. He was intelligent, a reader, a thinker, a master chess player, and he loved crossword puzzles. My father had a sense of humor, but he didn't laugh very often. When he did laugh, his laughter was hearty and loud. When in a good mood, he would play games with Scott and me. His favorite family games included Scrabble and Monopoly; we would also play checkers, chess, and card games. He would take my brother and me to the park to go sleigh riding in the winter or to the sandbox when the weather was nice. We would have picnics in the park during the summer months. Marty would pack a wicker basket with everything we needed, and she would set the picnic table with a tablecloth, napkins, plates, glasses and eating utensils. It was as if we were at the dinner table, only we had the beauty of nature surrounding us. During the summer months, I remember my father taking us to the pavilion in the park to make a fire so that we could toast marshmallows.

Based on the way my father conducted himself when he was around me, I never thought for a minute that he was nothing short of honest, loving, and caring; a man of high moral standards and character. I knew that he was big on appearances, but I really believed in him. Even though Scott and I wore old worn-out clothes, we had a nice place to live. We always had food to eat – even if it wasn't what we really wanted. We had each other, and my father made sure that our basic needs were met. However, as time passed, I started to notice some other traits of his personality; he was also a womanizer and a gambler. As I got older it became clear that my father had two personalities: one that he presented to the world, where he was an upstanding citizen, an intelligent and eloquent gentleman, and another one, that he mainly took on at home, where he was an angry, abusive and controlling man. In fact, one of my brothers called that side "the monster": he could turn on a dime from the gentleman outside to the monster at home.

Being with my Dad and Marty

As I mentioned before, my father had met "Marty," a rich white woman, during a political rally in Reading and they became romantically involved. My father was significantly older than she. At the time, I didn't understand who she was to my father. I just wanted to be with my Daddy. After we had moved into our new house, Marty's parents sent the Steinway piano to her - it had to be lifted through the second-floor window because it couldn't fit through the front door. Everything just seemed so magical, new and wonderful.

In my eyes, Marty was an amazing woman. She was beautiful and smart. She had a slender body with long light brown hair. Her hair nearly touched her butt when she let it down, but most of the time she pinned it up in a fancy hair-twist. She had fair white skin and brown eyes. She was soft-spoken, refined, talented and highly intelligent. She spoke fluent French, Creole, German and Russian. She was also an accomplished pianist. Marty was a loving, compassionate person, who cared for my brother and me as if we were her own.

My father married Marty in 1967. Scott and I attended the wedding. The pictures of the wedding speak volumes. Marty's lily-white family looked like dignitaries to me. Marty's father, who I referred to as "Pabby", was a surgeon. Her mother, who I referred to as "Mimi", was a surgical nurse. Her brother Richard, "Uncle Dick" was a medical doctor. I don't remember much about Marty's extended family (her aunts, uncles, and cousins), but a few of them were present at the wedding. In contrast, my father's mother "Grandma Hurtman" was a beautician and his grandmother did "day's work" for white folks. After the wedding, Marty was estranged from her family. The only family members who stayed in contact with her were her mother, father, and brother. Obviously, she paid a huge price to share her life with my father.

We got settled into the house that I thought Marty or her parents had bought, but I found out much later that Marty was renting the house. My brother Scott and I were enrolled in private schools – Green Street Friends and then Miquon. The Miquon School is an independent, parent-owned, elementary school located in Whitemarsh on the suburban outskirts of Philadelphia, Pennsylvania.

The schools we attended were predominantly white; I was the only kindergarten student of color in my class. I was bright, articulate and well mannered. However, I was a strong-willed little girl. Even at the tender age of five, I had a temper, and when I acted out in school for whatever reason, I was dealt with harshly by the school staff. I remember a time when the teacher told me to do something, and I thought I was being treated unfairly, so I refused. The principal was called to address the situation. He was a tall white man. Since I refused to move, when he arrived in the classroom, he picked me up, placed me over his shoulder, and carried me to the main office like a sack of potatoes. I kicked, cried, and screamed. When we arrived in the principal's office, I had to sit and wait for my father to pick me up. My brother attended the same school, and we used to catch the train home from school, but on this particular day he had to wait in the principal's office with me.

I knew my Dad was going to be extremely upset with me. He walked into the building and went straight to the principal's office to find out what had transpired. When my dad approached me, I could see the look of disapproval all over his face. In a stern voice he said, "Jackie, I want you to apologize for your behavior today." I turned and rendered an apology to the principal, and we left the building. As soon as we got in the car, my father told me to go straight to my room when I got home. That was the first time my father beat me with his belt.

When my father left our home in Reading, I didn't understand why. When he took us to Philly to be with him, I didn't know where my mother Maxine was or what she was doing while my brother and I were in Philadelphia. The first few years in Philadelphia were full of wonderful experiences with Dad and Marty. Marty was a brilliant woman, who had been exposed to the finer things in life. Accordingly, she intended to provide a similar upbringing for Scott and me. The fact that we were African-American children never seemed to faze her. She made sure that we were members of the library, the Franklin Institute (Philadelphia's science museum) and the Methodist Church, which is where she and my dad were married. She taught me to play the piano, the ukulele (a small guitar), and the recorder (similar to a flute). She made a wholesome lunch for my brother and me every day. We always sat down at the dining room table as a family for breakfast and dinner. We always joined hands to say grace before we ate and we had to ask to be excused in order to leave the dinner table. Marty taught us proper etiquette – no elbows on the table, place the napkin on your lap, use a fork and knife (never fingers). Talking with food in our mouths was unacceptable. The table had to be fully set before meals were served. We always had fresh hot meals and "The Golden Rule" was strictly enforced – "Do unto others as you would have them do unto you". Ironically, the word "lie" and the phrase "shut up" were not allowed to be used inside or outside the home. Marty and my Dad had great command of the "King's English" and they expected us to follow suit. Accordingly, we were taught to speak properly at all times. As a result, I was teased for sounding like a "white girl" when speaking among peers. My father was a community activist and a wannabe businessman; he started several businesses in Germantown, but all of them failed. Marty was an English teacher, specializing in adult education.

I was seven years old when my Dad brought a young college student to our house. This young woman, Joanne Demminson, lived in a house on the corner, just up the street from our house. She had three roommates who were college students as well. Joanne had a pudgy frame, curly light brown hair, very pale white skin and big legs. She became a regular visitor, and before I knew it, she was spending the night at our house, sleeping on the sofa.

My brother and I spent a lot of time playing in the park after school and on weekends. One Saturday afternoon we went outside to play; we had been outside for awhile, and I had to go to the bathroom. I ran home, entered the house, and I heard someone moaning. As I tiptoed upstairs, the sound became louder. I walked down the hallway to Dad and Marty's bedroom. I pushed the door open and saw Dad, Marty, and Joanne all in bed naked. I quickly ran back down the hallway, back down the stairs, and out the front door. I didn't even go to the bathroom but instead ran to find Scott to tell him about what just happened. When I found him, I told him but he didn't want to believe me. I said: "Scott it's true. Dad was in the bed with Joanne and Marty! When I walked in the house, I heard somebody moaning really loud. I couldn't imagine who it was, so I tiptoed upstairs and looked in their bedroom. I know they saw me." No one ever spoke a word about this afterward. We all acted like it didn't happen.

As previously stated, my father liked to gamble. He particularly took an interest in horse racing. Marty was a good wife and mother, so she stayed at home with Scott and me when he went out at night. My dad didn't want Marty to work outside the home, so she stopped teaching and became a full-time stay-at-home mom. Marty made sure dinner was prepared, our homework was done, and we were tucked in bed at a decent time. As kids, my brother and I weren't allowed to watch television except for educational programs such as *National Geographic* or *Wild Kingdom*. While Marty assumed responsibility for us kids, my father took time to gallivant with Joanne, and she followed him wherever he went, including to the Belmont Race Track. Joanne and Marty were allegedly friends, but I never could understand how Marty let this young college student come into our home, eat our food, and sleep with my father - her husband - right in front of us. I grew angry about the situation. My father was always preaching about "The Golden Rule" to us, and clearly he wasn't living up to it.

There was noticeable tension in the house. Joanne's presence was more frequent and grew more disturbing to me. One Saturday morning upon rising, I walked downstairs into the living room and caught my father pushing something into Joanne's vagina. She was sitting on the sofa with her legs open. My father was in front of her using what looked to me like a rubbery "thing" on her. As soon as I appeared, they both jumped to attention. My dad tried to hide the "thing" and Joanne covered herself with a blanket that had fallen to the floor. I asked Dad, "What are you doing?" and he gave me some lame explanation like he was giving Joanne a massage or something, but then in a stern voice he told me to go back upstairs. So, I did what he said and went straight to my brother's room on the third floor to tell him what just happened. And once again, no one ever spoke about this either!

Although Dad and Marty never engaged in loud arguments, I remember hearing my Dad talk to her in a stern disapproving tone. Marty would get upset, but she didn't argue; she seemed to be intimidated by my father. Every once in a while, I would catch a glimpse of what appeared to be an argument or a very intense conversation between Marty and Dad. I don't know for sure what they were arguing about, but one subject that I wished somebody would have said something about was "Joanne Demminson!" I really wanted somebody to say something to get her out of our lives. But everybody acted like it was perfectly normal for her to be there.

Marty was very health conscious. As years went by, it became apparent that Marty developed an eating disorder. She thought that certain foods created mental confusion, causing her to act weird, so she got to the point that she only ate certain foods at certain times during the day, in very small portions. When I was six or seven years old, she adopted a macrobiotic food regimen, which included a lot of brown rice, kasha, spinach, as well as other healthy foods, no sugar and very little salt. It just so happened that soon after Marty made the switch, I began to notice that she would leave her pocketbook on the hutch in the dining room. So on Saturday mornings, I would make sure to be the first one up, and I would take loose change from her purse. Since no one said anything about it, it became a pattern of mine to look for Marty's purse on Saturday and Sunday mornings so I could take her change. I didn't tell my brother about it until I had accumulated enough money for us to go to the hoagie (sandwich) shop to buy whatever we wanted to eat. I went to my brother and told him to come on – "Let's go get a hoagie!" He wanted to know where I got the money, so I told him. He smiled at my response. We walked along the "Indian Trail" of Fern Hill Park down the hill to the hoagie shop. I ordered a turkey and cheese hoagie, and Scott ordered ham and provolone, with the works – lettuce, tomatoes, onions, oil, vinegar, extra mayo, oregano, salt, and pepper. We got some french fries to go with our sandwiches. This was a real treat!!! It felt so good to share with my brother the money I had stolen. Once again, no one ever spoke a word about this. I never knew if Marty noticed that change was missing from her wallet every week, but neither she nor my father ever said a word about it.

My brother is three years older than I and was taught to look out for me. As kids, we went everywhere together, although he was always trying to get rid of me. We visited my mother Maxine and my grandmother "Mom" in Newark, New Jersey on certain holidays; we would ride the train alone together. As young as ages three and six, we were traveling with no adult supervision. Our father would take us to 30th Street Station in Philadelphia, purchase our tickets, and wait with us until the train arrived. My brother would hold my hand, and we would stick together. Thank God we never had any problems while on the train, and we always arrived safely in Newark. As soon as we would step off the train Maxine (my mother) and "Mom" (my grandmother) would be there to greet us. They would hug us real tight and comment on how much we had grown since the last time they saw us. We were very "proper" kids – we spoke well, we were well mannered and always quiet around adults. We were taught that kids were better seen and not heard.

My mother Maxine always took me to stay with her and my grandmother Nan always took Scott. Even though Scott and I knew that we were brother and sister (we look very much alike), when we were with Maxine and "Mom," a separation was put between us and we weren't treated like siblings. There was a distinction made that let us know that when we were with Maxine and "Mom" we weren't supposed to act like brother and sister. But we weren't sure why this difference was being made, and it only happened when we were with them. We always had a good time in Newark with our family, though. We were treated especially well. Maxine and "Mom" would buy us clothes and I would always get my hair washed and pressed. My grandmother "Mom" did my hair, and she always complained about the way *that white woman* wasn't combing my hair through to the root. It seemed that the only time my hair got washed was when I visited her. Getting my hair done made me feel clean and pretty.

My grandmother "Mom" had an apartment on Keer Avenue across the street from Weequahic Park. My mother Maxine lived in an apartment on Lyons Avenue, which wasn't very far from where my "Mom" lived. My brother and I would go back and forth between apartments. The food was sooo good. My grandmother would cook up fried chicken, fried fish, smothered pork chops, collard greens, cabbage – you name it – she cooked it, and man-o-man did it taste good. In Philadelphia, Marty didn't allow us to eat fried foods or sugar. In Newark, my grandmother allowed us to eat anything we wanted. She would bake whatever cakes and pies we wanted. And she would let us eat as much as we wanted. Returning to our home in Philadelphia was so hard for me. I cried every time I had to leave my mother and grandmother. I didn't tell them about Joanne and all the things that were going on with Dad and Marty. We didn't talk about it, and no one asked.

Jon Scott Hurtman

Scott was a good athlete; he played just about every sport – ice hockey, baseball, football, basketball, and tennis. He was good at whatever he did – just not good enough for Dad. No matter what Scott did, no matter how well he performed, Dad always found something to criticize him about. I vividly remember one summer afternoon we went to the baseball diamond at Fern Hill Park right across the street from our house. My father said that he wanted to help Scott with his swing. I went with Scott, one of his friends, and my Dad. My brother's friend served as a pitcher. Dad chastised Scott for not keeping his eyes on the ball. Every time the ball was pitched to my brother, he missed. Every time my brother swung the bat and missed the ball my father yelled at him. I felt so bad for my brother. I cheered him on and kept saying, "Come on Scottie, you can do it! Hit the ball!" My father had chastised him so badly that he had begun to cry. Finally, my father said to Scott, "If you hit the ball, I'll give you a dollar." The next time the ball was pitched to him, he hit the ball so hard that it went way outfield. I was so happy for Scott you would have thought that I won the money. I knew he could do it, but my father was so hard on him. Just hearing my father's voice made him nervous. As a result, my brother performed better when my father wasn't around.

Martha Newsome

Marty and Dad—wedding day 1967

Scott and Jackie with Santa

Dad, Jackie and Scott 1968

Easter Sunday 1970 -- Jackie and Scottie with Mom in Newark, NJ.

> "Moving on is a simple thing, what it leaves behind is hard."
>
> **~ Dave Mustaine**

CHAPTER 4

The Move to Newark

The last time I remember visiting my mother in Newark, I cried hysterically when it was time for me to leave. My brother and I waited for our father in my mother's apartment. When he arrived to pick us up to take us back to Philadelphia, he came inside to get our suitcases. We hugged my mother Maxine and her fiancé Vincent (my mother had become engaged to a man named Vincent Chavez; everybody called him "Vin") but all of a sudden I burst into tears. I cried and screamed; I didn't want to leave. My father pulled me along and told me to get in the car. I resisted. He pulled me with force. I was still crying when he placed me in the car, and I kept saying, "I don't want to go. Mommy, don't make me go. I want to stay with you." Eventually, my father drove off. Once I had simmered down a bit, my father gave me a stern look and said: "If you ever do that again you'll never see your mother!" Wow, I thought to myself. Would my father really keep me from seeing my mother?

It was August of 1972 when my mother Maxine and her fiancé Vin showed up at our house in Philadelphia unexpectedly. When they came in the house, my mother exchanged a few words with my father, and then she came into my room to speak with me about moving to New Jersey to live with her. I was nine years old. I was so excited; this is exactly what I had prayed for. I ran upstairs to talk to Scott about it. "Scott, come with me," I said anxiously. "Let's go!" I pleaded. He said "No. I'm not going. Girl, you go ahead!" I really didn't want to leave my brothers. By this time, Marty had given birth to my baby brother Joel; he was born the previous October, so he wasn't quite a year old.

I loved my brothers and really wanted to be with them; but the situation in Philly with my Dad, Marty, and Joanne was unbearable for me, and I thought that living with my mother would be better. So I left with Maxine and Vin! I would come back to visit my brothers in Philadelphia from time to time, though. We remained in touch through the years. My father always wanted me to be close to my brothers. He instilled in me that "I am my brothers' keeper."

The situation in Philly got worse and worse for my brother Scott. I would imagine that my father's insistence that Joanne live in the same house with him and his wife Marty might have had something to do with the problem. Scott told me that as soon as I left, Joanne moved into my room. Scott's room was in the attic, on the third floor. The only way for him to get to his room or out of his room was by going through my room. So when Joanne moved to my room, he had to pass by her all of the time. He told me that he caught Dad in bed with Joanne many times.

My younger brother Joel was the "golden child", as I always refer to him. He's the only legitimate child of us three. His mother Marty and our biological father John Hurtman were married when he was born. Joel arrived into the world with fair skin and good looks and was given freedoms that Scott never had. Joel was a precocious child, extremely active and highly intelligent. Marty adored her son, and Dad didn't want Marty to do anything but take care of him and his son. But, while Marty was at home taking care of Scott and Joel, Dad was out gallivanting with Joanne. After hearing more stories from Scott about where I'd just left, I thought it was best that I live with my mother.

The Child Died

I remember the day it happened -- my whole life changed. It was a cool autumn afternoon. I was nine years old, a fourth grader. I hurried home from school. It was raining, and the wind blew fiercely. I had worn a plaid skirt with a button-down white shirt, knee socks, and white shoes with brown stitching on the side. My umbrella was no match for the strong wind and rain, but I held on tight hoping to get home without getting struck by lightning. The clouds were thick, and the thunder was loud. It was a scary afternoon, but I made it home okay.

My mother had given me a key to the house where we lived, and I wore it around my neck. I used the key to unlock the door. I entered and locked the door from the inside. It was one of those deadbolts that had to be locked and unlocked from the inside and outside using a key. It was a two-family house, and we lived on the second floor; my grandmother "Mom" lived on the first floor. I believe it was close to three o'clock when I got home from school that day. I was cold and wet, so I went straight to my room to take off my clothes. I could hear the television in the other room. Vin was still at home; he worked nights at Ford Motor Company as an assembly-line worker. I thought he was running late for work, but he didn't seem to be in a rush to leave the house. I decided to put on my pajamas – when I opened my bedroom door, Vin was standing there. He was about 6 feet 4 inches tall. He had on light blue boxer underwear and a white V-neck short sleeve undershirt. He had a slim build and very hairy legs. He said, "Hi Jackie. You got pretty wet today. Come in my room; you can get in bed with me. I'll warm you up." I said "Okay" and didn't think there was anything wrong with getting into bed with him because my father John Hurtman used to cuddle up with me when I didn't feel well, and he never did anything that made me feel uncomfortable. Vin liked to watch cartoons, and so did I. That afternoon cartoons were on television.

I remember being light hearted and happy. Vin got in the bed and pulled back the covers and said: "Get in." I got in the bed, and he covered me; he moved my small frame close to him until his body was touching mine. He turned me on my side and wrapped his arms around me. He asked me if I was warm and I said, "Yes." I was focused on the cartoons and felt comfortable for the moment. And then, I felt his hand on my leg. Right then, I knew his touch didn't feel right, but I didn't tell him to stop. He moved his hand up toward my panties and then began to stroke my vagina with his finger. He whispered, "Don't tell your mother about this." I FROZE! I didn't move; it was as if I was paralyzed. He was rubbing his penis on my butt and rubbing my vagina with this finger. His hands were all over my young body. I don't remember what happened after that; it's a blur...

That was the first time "it" happened. That was the day the little girl inside me died. That was the day I stopped wanting to go outside to play; instead, I would look out the window and watch other children on the block play tag, hopscotch, and jump rope. I used to love to play outside, but now I felt dirty. I thought everyone could tell what was happening to me. Was "it" my fault? As I looked out the window, tears rolled from my eyes down my cheeks. I didn't play outside anymore. My mother's fiancé Vin created his own sex game that he played with me indoors. He liked to chase me around and then pounce on me. That was his fun and our secret.

I did well in school. Prior to moving to Newark, New Jersey, I had attended private schools and public schools in predominantly white, affluent communities. I continued to perform well in school even after being sexually abused. A few days after being molested by Vin, I told my mother that I didn't like the school she had put me in; the name of the school was Alexander Street School. It was located in the Vailsburg section of the city. I told my mother that I wasn't learning anything new. The next week my mother transferred me to a Catholic school called Saint Antoninus, located on 9th Street. Vin drove me to school every day, and I had to catch the bus home after school. Often times he would make a pit-stop at a local bar to have a few shots of liquor before dropping me off at school. I would wait in the car while he was in the bar. I wasn't sure if my mother Maxine knew that he drank liquor early in the morning, but I never mentioned it. I stopped talking to Vin and became very withdrawn. I was angry and hurting. I cried a lot, but I didn't tell my mother what Vin was doing to me until a couple years later.

Telling My Mother

It was a Friday evening. I was busy cleaning my room; I always kept my room clean. This particular evening, I was cleaning and changing my furniture around. My mother Maxine was at home, and she said something to me as she walked passed my room. During this period of my life, when I was at home I was always angry and would go days without speaking to my mother and Vin unless I had to. Anyway, since my mother had addressed me, I said *"Mother"* - I always refer to her as "mother" – not "mommy" or "mom" – *"There's something I think you should know. I realize that you're about to get married to Vin, but I think you should know who you're about to marry."* It was hard for me to tell my mother the truth but I thought she needed to know. I actually thought that she might change her mind about marrying him if she knew what he had done to me. Maybe if she knew, she'd make him leave. So with all the courage I had, I nervously began to speak. I said in a rather low voice, "Mother, Vin has been touching me; he's having sex with me. Whenever you're not around, he has sex with me." My mother responded quickly and harshly, "You're lying Jackie! You're just jealous!" I couldn't believe my ears. "Why would I lie to you about something like that? Why would I be thinking about sex at my age?" (I was eleven years old at the time.) I just moved here to be with you, and he did this to me. I'm only telling you for your own good. Go ahead and marry him! I just wanted you to know who you were getting ready to marry. He's a child molester!" I was yelling and crying at the same time. "That's why I hate you! I HATE YOU!" I slammed my bedroom door in her face, fell out on my bed and cried. I cried for a long time, but no one consoled me!

When I was by myself, I would cry all the time. I felt so isolated and alone. When my mother called me a liar it was like someone stabbed me in my heart with a butcher knife. The worst part was that I had to continue to live with my abuser and my mother – two people I couldn't stand. I shut down emotionally. I didn't speak to them unless I had to. I was very unhappy. When I left Philadelphia to live in Newark, little did I know that I was going from the frying pan into the fire!

It was unfathomable to me that the adults around me made such poor decisions for themselves and hurt the children that they professed to love in the process. How can thinking adults engage in such deplorable behavior around children, lie to them, to the extent that their lies become their truth and then expect the children to live out those lies? Can you even imagine that? Several months later, my mother Maxine married Vin, who was twenty years older than she.

Shortly after the wedding, my mother announced to me that she had changed my name. She showed me that my birth certificate had been altered; she had used white-out to change Hurtman to "Chavez." I said, "How could you do that?! You know good and well he's my abuser, and you actually changed my name without even talking to me about it." I was furious. I told my mother that I was not going to write the name Chavez. "You can't make me either!" I exclaimed. She insisted and said that she was going to change the records at school so that my name would be registered as Jacquelin Chavez. There was simply no regard for how I felt about the matter, so I relented and started using the name Chavez. I screamed and shouted and let my mother know once again just how much I hated her. I yelled "You make me sick! I hate you!" Life just continued on as if everything was all right.

Scott Comes to Newark

Things had gotten really bad for Scott in Philadelphia. My father was verbally and physically abusive to him. I think Scott was 15 years old when he finally had enough. There was a major confrontation that occurred between Scott and Dad. One day Joanne made up a story and told my father a lie about something Scott did. Instead of my father asking Scott what happened, he believed Joanne. He must have thought that he was going to beat up on Scott as he had done in the past, but this time turned out to be very different. Dad approached Scott as if he was going to punch him in his chest, Scott blocked the punch, grabbed his arm, and said, "You're not going to hit me this time... no, not ever again!" Dad was shaken; he could see that Scott was enraged. Scott ran upstairs to his room picked up a steel bar from his weight set and started swinging the bar wildly. He swung hard enough to puncture the walls; he even used his bare fist to punch huge holes in the walls. As he swung, he called my father every curse word he could think of "YOU MOTHERFUCKING SON OF A BITCH... FUCK YOU!" He cried and lashed out in total anger. The bedroom windows were wide open; anybody near the house could hear him. Dad didn't dare come upstairs to try to stop him. I guess he realized that day that at his age he was no match for Scott. That was a turning point in my brother's life. He had clearly had enough of Dad's foolishness.

That night Scott called "Mom" and asked her to come get him, but she didn't come right away. Scott called just about every day. He would go to a pay phone to call "Mom" – back then pay telephones could be found on major street corners. I remember my grandmother "Mom" telling my mother Maxine that Scott had called her "collect." It was a cold, rainy fall night; Scott was angry and crying and begged my grandmother "Mom" to come get him but still she didn't come. One Saturday morning when no one was at home Scott called again and said, "Please come now, no one is at the house; you've got to come get me." So my mother Maxine drove her husband's station wagon to Philadelphia to get him. While Scott waited for Maxine, he gathered up all his trophies, tennis rackets, a few clothes, and his dog, Mitzi. He was ready to leave when Maxine arrived. Scott left without saying good-bye.

It was Scott's first day in Newark when my mother Maxine and grandmother "Mom" called us to meet in the dining room of my grandmother's house, which was on the first floor of our two-family house. We all stood up around the table. I don't know who started the conversation; I think it was my mother Maxine who said: "I just want you to know that you're not brother and sister." She said to Scott, "Mom" [in reality our grandmother] is your mother." Then she turned to me and said: "Jackie, I'm your mother." I immediately blurted out "So Scott's my uncle?!" Scott and I looked at each other in total disbelief, but nothing more was said about it at that time.

The day after Scott arrived in Newark, my father, Marty, and little brother Joel showed up at our house. Very few words were exchanged; my father had come to get the dog. Mitzi was Scott's dog. My father knew that Scott loved his dog, but that was his way of retaliating. There wasn't a big fight; my grandmother "Mom" told Scott to let them take the dog. Once they had put the dog on its leash, they left. Scott was heart-broken but within a few weeks, my grandmother "Mom" got Scott a full-blooded German Shepherd that he named Bianca.

Shortly after my mother Maxine made the announcement that Scott wasn't my brother – that she's my mother and that "Mom" (Miss Nan, the woman I referred to as my grandmother) is his, I confronted her and wanted to know who our father was. It was a Saturday afternoon, and we were the only two in the second-floor apartment of the house. I asked her if Dad was the father of both of us. She said "No!"

"Who is my father?" I asked.

She said, "Joe Queen is your father, and Bill Foster is Scott's father."

"So where are these people? I want to meet them!"

"They're dead." "Really Mother? Is that the best story that you can come up with? Conveniently, they're both dead! Sure they're dead because they don't exist! You really expect me to believe that some man by the name of Joe Queen is my father? And who did you say is Scott's father?"

"Bill Foster" she stated in a somewhat subdued tone. She tried to maintain her composure, but I was yelling at the top of my lungs.

"Well, did you ever tell Scott who his father 'really' is?"

"No!" she responded.

"Why not?" I asked.

"Because he never asked."

"Well, I'm going to tell him! -- This is the most outrageous story I've ever heard. You really want me to believe that some man you've never mentioned before by the name of Joe Queen is my father, and he just happens to be dead?!"

Even though I was in a state of total disbelief, I continued to demand answers. "So when did he die?"

"I don't know Jackie. Last year sometime... I think."

"Oh, just last year – how convenient!"

By this point, I was outraged and yelled, "You're a pathetic liar. I hate you! I HATE YOU!"

I don't know what was worse for me, being sexually violated by my mother's fiancé (now husband), or my mother accusing me of lying about it, or her telling me that my brother is my uncle... Or that we have different fathers, and they're both dead.

Jon Scott aka Scottie

The house in Newark was a two-family house with a full basement and an attic. My grandmother "Mom" lived on the first floor, and Scott moved into the second bedroom on the first floor. My mother Maxine, her husband Vin and I lived on the second floor. By the time Scott moved to Newark, my mother and Vin had been married for about a year. They got married when I was eleven years old. Everyone was supposed to believe that Scott was my mother's brother. This was when things started to get really crazy for me. First of all, there was no way that I was going to believe that the person I grew up referring to as my brother is now my uncle. But, everybody around me accepted this, even Scott.

After Scott had moved to Newark, there was what could be described as an "out-of-control normalcy" that existed within our home. Soon after "the meeting" when my mother made the announcement that Scott's not my brother, I went to his room to talk to him about the situation. I said, "Scott you know you're my brother right?! I don't care what they say. I know you're my brother!!" He said, "Girl go away. I don't want to talk about it. Will you just leave me alone!" Scott was the quiet one, and I was the boisterous one -- at home that is. In public, I was poised, polished and polite. I played the part my parents wanted me to play in public but behind closed doors, at home, it was a very different story. I was angry and defiant.

63

Scott and I saw each other every day, but we led separate lives. Scott played tennis and was very talented at the sport. He practiced all of the time; he ate and drank tennis. As a young African-American tennis player in the Vailsburg section of Newark, he received a lot of attention. This was during the 1970s when tennis was a lily-white sport. Althea Gibson and Arthur Ashe were the only two African-American professional tennis players at the time. Scott was on the rise, following in their footsteps; he actually had an opportunity to play tennis with both of them. By the time Scott was a senior in high school he was the captain of the tennis team at Newark Academy, a prestigious private school located in Livingston, New Jersey. He was recruited to attend the school because of his athletic ability. Scott was the only black tennis player on the team and only one of few students of color at the school.

Scott was a good kid – nice, quiet, polite and a super athlete. He was thin, tall, with golden brown skin, a nice sized afro and buck teeth. Eventually, my grandmother "Mom" got braces for his teeth, which he wore for several of his teen years. He didn't wear his emotions on his sleeve as I did but I knew he wasn't happy unless he was winning on the tennis court. Unfortunately, Scott severely injured his right knee while playing in a senior pick-up basketball game. He continued to compete in tennis tournaments on the injured knee. He was just that good; he was able to win even playing with an injured knee.

After graduating high school, Scott went on to play tennis at Texas Christian University. However, during his sophomore year at TCU, he completely tore the meniscus on the inside and outside of his knee. He then transferred to Ohio State University for his junior year. While playing a practice match he fell and tore his ACL (anterior cruciate ligament) and PCL (posterior cruciate ligament) in the same knee, which required a total knee reconstruction. In an effort to break his fall, he tore a tendon in the thumb of his right hand, which is his racquet hand. His thumb also required surgery. Scott's tennis career ended right there. Neither "Mom" nor Maxine ever set foot on either campus while Scott was there.

Vin and Maxine-wedding 1974

Vin and Maxine

John Scott age 14

Scott's many trophies

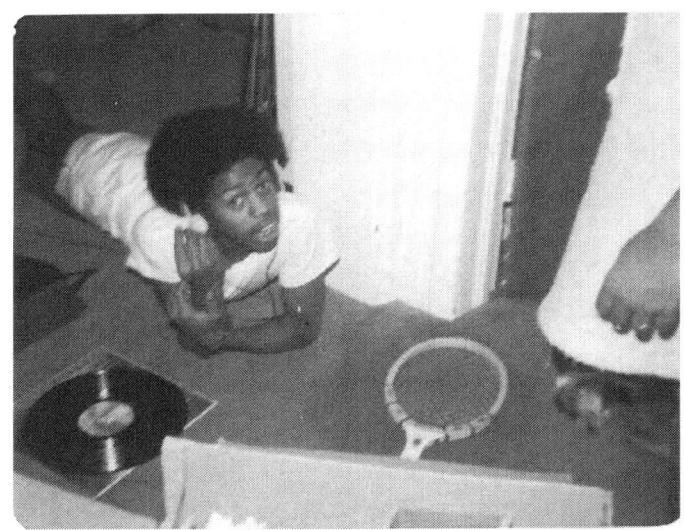

Scott listening to music

Scott after surgery

> "It is a poverty to decide that a child must die
> so that you may live as you wish."
>
> ~ **Mother Teresa**

CHAPTER 5

Terminating Life

The first time I had consensual sex I was 13 years old. I went to the youth games; I played tennis for the city of Newark. All of the various teams (basketball, baseball, volleyball, track and field, tennis, etc.) from across the country stayed on the campus of Tufts University. I met a boy who was 16 years old. After competing during the day, I went to his room one night. We started kissing. He wanted to have sex, so I did it. The boy was from Chicago. When I returned home, I spoke to him on the phone a few times, but his interest in me soon fizzled. Shortly after that, I met a boy who lived in my neighborhood and became sexually involved with him. Before I knew it, I was pregnant. It was just that simple!

When I missed my period, I panicked. I didn't want to tell my mother - during this phase of my life, I was extremely angry at her and didn't communicate unless I had to. I decided to call my father to ask him for help. When I spoke to him, he asked me if I had told my mother and I said: "No, I didn't want her to know." One of my mother's favorite sayings was "some things are better left unsaid." This was one of those "things." My father told me to give him a few days, and he would get back to me. When he did, he told me that Joanne (his mistress) had made an appointment for me to have an abortion. There was no discussion about whether or not I wanted to keep my baby. I remember traveling to Philadelphia on a Friday afternoon after school, and on Saturday morning, we got up bright and early to drive to New York City. My father, Joanne and I went to the abortion clinic. My father paid cash for the abortion and waited for me in the reception area while the fetus inside me was sucked from my uterus and killed.

70

"I feel the greatest destroyer of peace today is 'Abortion,' because it is a war against the child... A direct killing of the innocent child, 'Murder' by the mother herself... And if we can accept that a mother can kill even her own child, how can we tell other people not to kill one another? How do we persuade a woman not to have an abortion? As always, we must persuade her with love..."

~ Mother Teresa

As I reflect, aside from the sexual abuse, the most horrifying experience in my life was my very first abortion. The sexual abuse had already torn my soul to shreds, now the remaining pieces of my life were being pulverized. From that experience grew some of my darkest moments. I had made up my mind to keep the abortion a secret. I didn't have sex for a while after that. However, eventually I did, and before long I was pregnant again. I will never forget how I found out.

One evening after my mother came home from work we went to the Woodbridge Mall in Woodbridge, New Jersey. I hadn't eaten much on that particular day. We had just arrived at the mall and walked past Sbarro's Pizzeria and all of a sudden everything faded to black. I fainted! When I regained consciousness, I had water on my face. My mother had water in her hand and was clearly concerned. I remember trying to get up as quickly as I could. People were staring at me. I was very embarrassed.

My mother made a doctor's appointment for me right away. The next day I had blood work done, a urinalysis and God only knows what other tests were done. The outcome – I was pregnant. My mother made an appointment for an abortion. I was 15 when I had my second abortion. There was no discussion about whether or not I wanted to keep my baby. I had to save face for the family. Childbirth as a teenager was unacceptable. It didn't seem to matter that a part of me was being executed without my permission. Again, although I was polite and poised in public, at home I was a terror on a newer level now. Quietly, I hated everybody, especially myself. But in public, I spoke softly. I was polite. I did well in school. I did well at most things I set out to accomplish, but inside I felt totally empty. I felt miserable, alone, lost, abandoned, and invisible. My favorite song during this time was entitled "To Be Invisible" by Gladys Knight. The words of the song went like this:

To Be Invisible

Will be my claim- - to fame
A girl with no name
that way I won't have to feel the pain
Indispensable
just a plain-- old human being
Today don't mean a thing
in a world, that's so mean
A world that seems not for me
so privately
I'll be invisible
That way I won't have to explain a thing
If you know what I mean
I won't even have to be here on the scene
It's so ridiculous
of the strife and bliss
To go right on through,
right on through me to have missed

All the things that hurt you so
No one would ever know
They'd never know.
Life's so preciously
Just don't seem to be
as free as they claim freedom to be
Things are going fast
To have found it all in the past
To have to take what, you can get
Sure can make a heart upset
Inconspicuous
I must behave myself
For somebody else
that may have a little fame, fortune, and wealth
It's so ridiculous
of the strife and the bliss
to go right on through
right on through me to have missed.

All the world seems not for me
So privately
I'll be invisible
that way I won't have to explain a thing
If you know what I mean
I won't even have to be here
on the scene
It's so ridiculous
for the strife and the bliss
To go right on through
Right on through me to have missed

All the things that hurt you so
No one would ever know
naw naw naw they'd never know
life so preciously
just don't seem to me
as free as they claim freedom to be
Oh Oh Oh
Things are going fast
to have found it all in the past
to have to take what you can get
sure can make a heart upset
so I'll be invisible
invisible
invisible
invisible

I used to look in the mirror while listening to this song and cry my heart out. I was hurting deep down in my soul. Yet, my family acted like everything was all right, and the secrets remained hidden. No one spoke the truth; as I said, my mother's favorite saying was, "some things are better left unsaid." I had other subsequent abortions that are a blur. I was sexually active and extremely fertile. I didn't use birth control. Maybe I had my own private death wish, and since I didn't have the courage to take my own life, I subconsciously participated in the death of the tiny life that grew inside me. I just didn't care.

During my senior year of high school, my mother's husband Vin was diagnosed with pancreatic cancer. He was given six months to live. At the time, I attended Marylawn of the Oranges, an all-girls parochial high school located in South Orange, New Jersey. I was a bright student, always eager to learn. I applied myself and did very well. A couple of my courses were independent study courses. As a result of Vin's diagnosis, my mother thought it would be better for me to move to Georgia to be with family so that I wouldn't have to deal with the situation at home. My mother made a decision to care for Vin at home. In my mind, it was clear that she had "again" chosen him over me. In late October 1980, I transferred to Baker County High School in Newton, Georgia. This was the first time I attended a co-ed high school. I could have graduated in December of 1980 because I had fulfilled the requirements to graduate but I stayed in school and graduated in June 1981. Even though I had straight A's and the highest cumulative average, I was not the valedictorian of my graduating class because I had not attended the school for a full year. Vin died in January of 1981. My mother bought a plane ticket so that I could attend his funeral.

Just prior to Vin's death, my mother Maxine and Vin purchased one acre of land in Newton, Georgia from a family member. Then they purchased a double-wide trailer with the intention of moving there before Vin died. However, Vin was too ill to travel. Immediately after Vin's funeral my grandmother "Mom" put the house in Newark up for sale. Once the house was sold, my grandmother retired from her job as a supervisor at a sewing factory and my mother Maxine resigned from her job at Bankers Trust located in New York City. Any furniture that they decided not to take with them, they gave to family and friends. Scott and I were not considered in this life-altering decision. "Mom" and Maxine moved into the trailer in 1981. My grandmother "Mom" lived there until the day she died.

> "Living with integrity means: Not settling for less than what you know you deserve in your relationships. Asking for what you want and need from others. Speaking your truth, even though it might create conflict or tension. Behaving in ways that are in harmony with your personal values. Making choices based on what you believe, and not what others believe."
>
> **~ Barbara De Angelis**

CHAPTER 6

"Olan" - "O": Orlando L. Covington

I met Orlando L. Covington - better known as "Olan" but I called him "O'- through a childhood friend named Linda Williams. I met Linda as soon as I moved to Newark in 1972 when I was nine years old. She lived on Ricord Street two doors down from me in Newark.

I left Georgia after graduating high school to attend Pennsylvania State University. I started the year at Penn State but after a horrible initiation experience into a sorority, I transferred to Albany State College in Albany (the nearest city to Newton, Georgia). As soon as I finished my exams, in June 1981, I traveled by bus to visit my aunt in East Orange, New Jersey. When I arrived, I let Linda know. A few days after my arrival, Linda told me that she wanted to introduce me to somebody. She told me that she had met some people at Ramapo College, her alma mater, and there was a guy that she wanted me to meet. One day Linda came by to pick me up, and we drove to meet up with her friends, Mike and Annie. We ended up taking a ride in Mike's car. Annie, Linda and I were in the car with him when we rode up to Paterson, New Jersey to meet two other friends of hers, Richard and Olan. They both jumped in the car. Annie and Richard sat in the front with Mike; Olan sat in the back with Linda and me.

We were all packed in Mike's car when "O" pulled out a foil package containing a white powder. He started breaking up the clumps of white powder using a matchbook cover. He asked me if I wanted some and I replied "No, thank you. I don't get high." Other than trying marijuana a few times, prior to this I did not get high. He said "Oh. Okay. No problem." He made a comment about my soft voice and then passed the cocaine along to Linda. Without hesitation, she took a hit, then looked at me and said "More for me!"

It didn't bother me to be around drugs or in a car with people doing drugs. Perhaps it was my ignorance; I was just happy to be on the scene because I knew I was the baby of the bunch. Linda was three years older than I, so everybody in the car with us was, at least, three years my senior as well.

Eventually, we ended up at Annie and Richard's apartment. They lived together in a one-bedroom apartment in Newark. There wasn't much furniture in the apartment, so we all sat around on the floor talking – they continued to pass the drugs around. I was listening intently but didn't talk much. "O" invited me to talk with him in the bedroom and I accepted. He commented that I didn't talk much. "You're the quiet type." He moved in close to kiss me and before I knew it he had started to unfasten my pants. The kiss was long and passionate. He was noticeably aroused. He took off his clothes, and so did I. We made passionate love like I had never experienced before. He was tall, dark and handsome. His body was strong; he had a slim build that was all muscle. He was gentle – and what a beautiful body! After spending a few hours together, he drove me to my aunt's house. That was the beginning of our relationship.

After that, we spent every day together. "O" was the first man to wine and dine me. He took me out to dinner regularly. He took me shopping for clothes, and he kept lots of money in his pocket. It was obvious that he didn't earn an honest living, but I didn't care. I felt my whole life was one big lie, so I really didn't care about adding more to an already fraudulent life. "O" had no idea about my life story. Actually, I was still trying to figure out my identity. To "O" I was a "proper young lady" from Georgia on summer break from school, who happened to be friends with his former school mate Linda.

"O" was very nice to me – loving, attentive, and protective. Prior to meeting "O", I had never been to Jersey City, New Jersey, which is where he lived. He stayed in the basement apartment of his parent's house. His mother and father were married, and he had four brothers and one sister. Within our first two months of dating, "O" started talking about us getting an apartment together.

My summer break was coming to an end, and I was supposed to return to college in Georgia, but I really enjoyed being with "O." He had charisma, strength, and confidence. What I admired most was the fact that he had a family – a mother, father, sister and brothers – and he wanted to be with me. I didn't have a job. I didn't have a plan – other than to return to school because that's what I was supposed to do. But, I really wanted to be with "O" and he wanted to be with me. He said he would put up the money if I would use my name to get the apartment. So, on September 1, 1982, we moved into an apartment on Sixth Avenue in Newark; the same apartment building that Annie and Richard lived in. I didn't return to school.

"O" didn't press me to get a job -- we hung out and had fun. We slept on a twin-sized box spring and mattress that we put on the bedroom floor – no frame, no dresser or chest of drawers – just lots of love and lovemaking. Little by little, we purchased furniture. One of my fondest memories of my time with "O" was when we would sit in the living room together. He would sit on the sofa; I would sit on the floor between his legs. He would brush my hair – he actually liked to play with my hair, and it thoroughly relaxed me.

"O" was well respected by his peers. He had a strong, powerful presence. He didn't really talk a lot either unless he was high. I didn't understand "street life" or the life of a hustler and drug dealer. I was naïve. But "O" kept the money flowing, so I didn't care. A few months into the relationship, I got pregnant. I had been taking birth control pills, so I was upset to be pregnant again. I told "O" right away. We talked about it and decided not to have the baby. This was abortion number ___? I'd lost count and "O" had no idea; he thought I was a "good girl." Well, I was a good girl. I just had some family secrets that haunted every aspect of my life. Somehow, I held it together. I put on appearances. Anyway, I had the abortion and carried on with my life.

When I was 21, I got pregnant again. With the second pregnancy, I actually thought I was constipated at first. Pregnancy was the furthest thing from my mind because I had been taking birth control pills regularly. When I missed my period, I bought a home pregnancy test, and it turned out positive. I asked "O" if he wanted the baby. He told me flat out: "You're not gonna kill another baby of mine." I am forever grateful to "O" for declaring that he wanted me to keep the baby. Bringing a life into the world changed my life.

Once, when "O" and I lived together, my father and younger brother Joel came to visit me. My father had a brief but pleasant conversation with "O." Some time later I explained to "O" that I wasn't certain that the man he met is my father. "O" said emphatically, "Jackie, that's your father." I never went into detail with "O" about my past. I kept the secret.

It was Mother's Day when I announced to my mother Maxine and grandmother "Mom" that I was three months pregnant. My grandmother was very upset about the news. She said, "You just ruined my Mother's Day." She followed-up with, "Was that supposed to be good news?!" I was crushed. I simply responded by saying, "I'm sorry you feel that way. I thought you would be happy for me." Next, my mother got on the phone and said, "Well, if you're gonna keep the baby you're going to have to take care of it just like I took care of mine. I'm not going to babysit." I responded by saying, "Yes, mother, I will take care of *my* baby." When the conversation ended, I hung up the phone and cried. I told "O" what happened, and he promised that he would always take care of his baby.

During the nine months of pregnancy, my relationship with "O" changed significantly. He spent more and more time in Jersey City at his mother's house. We didn't have sex very often. One day during my sixth month of pregnancy, I came home to a padlocked apartment. We were evicted.

"O" said that he would pay the rent but one month rolled into the next, and we kept getting more and more behind. "O" was running the street and I had a minimum wage job at an insurance company, where I performed data entry tasks and filing. The day that I came home to find a dead bolt on the door, we were three months behind in rent. So there I was standing outside while my few belongings were locked inside. The landlord agreed to allow me to move my furniture out of the apartment but only gave me 24 hours to do it. I think he felt sorry since I was pregnant. I contacted "O" and he had his friends help him move all of the items onto a small truck he rented. We moved to "O"'s mother's house in Jersey City where we stayed in the basement apartment.

My mother Maxine wasn't happy about my relationship with "O" much less that I was living with his family; so a few weeks later I contacted my Aunt Pat, who lived in Piscataway, New Jersey at the time, to ask her if I could stay with her until I found an apartment. She was kind enough to let me stay with her. "O" acted upset when I told him that I decided to leave his mother's house but I think he was probably relieved, he wouldn't have to worry about me or the baby that was on the way. I stayed at my aunt's house for three or four weeks and commuted back and forth to work by train. During this time, I looked for an apartment in the Newark/East Orange area. I wanted to live closer to my job which was located in East Orange on Evergreen Place.

Fortunately, it didn't take me long to find an apartment, but I was short on cash. My aunt helped me with money toward the security deposit, and in no time, I was moving into my new apartment. I was seven and a half months pregnant so I knew I had to get my apartment cleaned and ready for my baby. I called "O" to let him know that I had found an apartment and needed his help to move our belongings from his mother's house to the new apartment. This was when it became crystal clear to me that "O" was really upset about me leaving his mother's house. When I arrived to retrieve my belongings from his house, he hardly spoke to me, and he begrudgingly helped me load the furniture onto the U-Haul truck I rented. Once we got everything onto the truck, he turned to me and said, "You're on your own!" I was shocked, hurt, and felt abandoned. However, I knew that I didn't have time to waste. I was on the clock; the U-Haul truck had to be returned within 24 hours. I called my friend, Angela, to ask her to help me. I drove the truck to the apartment and Angela met me there. Thank God she showed up right away. She and I (baby belly and all) moved everything into the apartment. She kept telling me that I shouldn't lift anything but my response was, "If I don't do it then who will?!" So we proceeded to do what had to be done.

> "Let the light of love enlighten the whole world. Let the power of love overpower all the evils."
>
> **~ Debasish Mridha**

CHAPTER 7

Welcome to Motherhood

My father, Joanne and my brother Joel came to my new apartment to spend Thanksgiving with me. By this time my father and Marty were separated. I was so happy to have them with me. Otherwise, I would have been alone. "O" and I still weren't talking to each other very often. I was 22 years old, nine months pregnant, and ready to deliver my baby. I prepared the traditional Thanksgiving meal: turkey, stuffing, string beans, macaroni and cheese, candied yams, rice, corn bread, sweet potato pies and, of course, Kool-Aid. I was complaining about my back hurting, but I kept moving. I really enjoyed having my father and brother there. Joel must have been 13 years old at the time. They left late that night. I spent Friday and Saturday cleaning the apartment. Just before my father left, he told me that I looked like I was going to have the baby any day now. I didn't think he was right, but on Sunday, November 25, 1984, I went into labor. My water broke around noon; I was at home alone. I had an urge to urinate but before I could get to the bathroom a flood of water flowed down my legs. I called "O" to let him know. He seemed concerned. With a sense of urgency in his voice, he said: "Call the doctor right away and call me back." I called my doctor to explain what just happened. The doctor strongly suggested that I get to the hospital as soon as possible. I didn't have a car. "O" was in Jersey City at his mother's house. Since he didn't have a car, he wanted me to call for an ambulance to take me to the hospital. I wasn't going do that so I called my friend Linda; she had a car, and I knew she would help me. It didn't take Linda long to arrive at my door. When she arrived I was still packing my travel bag with items I thought I would need at the hospital. Linda fussed at me because she thought I was moving too slowly. Given the circumstance, I was very calm. I remember telling Linda that I didn't want to get to the hospital too soon before the baby is born because I didn't want to have a c-section; I wanted to deliver my baby naturally.

We arrived at Saint Michael's Hospital in Newark, New Jersey a little after 4:00 p.m. As soon as I walked through the doors I heard wild screams coming from one of the labor rooms. I looked at Linda and said, "I do not want to sound like that." I was scared to death. I thought to myself – How painful is this going to be? We proceeded to the labor room. I was given a gown and was told to disrobe and prepare for delivery. I laid on the bed with my feet in stirrups. Linda stayed with me as the nurse hooked straps around my belly to monitor my contractions. "O" and his friend Mike finally arrived. "O" kissed my forehead and asked me how I was doing – just then a contraction hit. I grabbed "O"'s hand and squeezed it tight. I didn't want to scream - not yet - and this was the first contraction I felt. Again, I thought to myself, this is only the beginning of the pain. I breathed quickly – in and out – and squeezed "O"'s hand even harder. When the contraction subsided, I released "O"'s hand. He was very glad that I did. As he massaged his fingers, he said, "Girl, you squeezed my hand so tight, you almost broke my fingers."

Everybody was hungry except for me. "O" and Mike went to Burger King to get something to eat. Linda searched for a vending machine within the hospital and wasn't gone long. When she returned, she had a bag of potato chips and a can of soda. I was starting to have another contraction. The doctor had arrived at this point. He and the nurse told me that I needed to bear down the next time I have a contraction. Evidently, I was pushing as if I was having a bowel movement and not bearing down correctly to push the baby out. Within minutes, I started to feel another contraction hit. This time, I did just what I was told. I pushed really hard! But then the doctor told me to stop so they could roll my bed across the hall to the delivery room. As soon as I was situated in the delivery room, the doctor told me to push as hard as I could the next time I have a contraction. That's exactly what I did. Jasmine was born at 7:46 p.m. She had a birthmark on her left cheek. The nurse cleaned her and laid her on my chest. When I looked to the right, guess who was peering through the windowpane of the double-doors? It was "O."

Even though Jasmine's father and I weren't married when she was born, I gave Jasmine his last name. He visited me every day for the three days that I was in the hospital after Jasmine's birth. When "O" came to pick us up from the hospital, he brought clothes for the baby with him. He was so proud and happy on that day. I dressed Jasmine in one of the new outfits and "O" drove us straight to his mother's house in Jersey City. We stayed there a few days and then went to East Orange to my apartment. Before I knew it, "O" was staying with us overnight on a frequent basis. My relationship with him had changed, though, and my hope of a stable family with him had faded.

When Jasmine was six weeks old, I had to return to work. I thought "O"'s mother would be willing to babysit for me during the day since she kept other people's children, but that didn't happen. I'll never forget the evening I asked Mama Covington if she would babysit for me. She told me that she had to speak to "O" about it. Unfortunately, he refused to talk to her. When "O" came to pick Jasmine and me up to drive us home, I asked him to talk to his mother about babysitting for us. For some reason, he didn't want to do it. He and his mom exchanged a few words but ultimately Mama Covington refused to babysit. "O" went out the back door and down the stairs into the basement. I asked Mama Covington if I could use her telephone. She said, "Yes." I called my grandmother "Mom" in front of her. I explained the situation to "Mom" and asked her if I could bring Jasmine to stay with her until I was able to get a reliable babysitter, someone I could trust. She said, "Yes." That time "Mom" didn't hesitate, she didn't stutter, she just said, "YES!"

I was so happy that she said "yes" but now I had to figure out how I was going to get Jasmine to Georgia without telling "O." Since "O" didn't stay with me every night, one weekend I told him that I was going to visit my aunt in Piscataway. He didn't think anything of it, so I went ahead and bought a plane ticket. Within a few days, Jasmine and I were headed to Georgia. I left Jasmine with my grandmother and returned to New Jersey the next day. It wasn't easy for me to leave Jasmine but when I considered the alternative I knew she would be better off with "Mom" than with anyone else. Plus "Mom" didn't charge me one red cent. When "O" finally showed up at the apartment Jasmine was gone. He asked me where she was, and I told him that I had taken her to my aunt's house to stay for a while. I think he believed me.

"O" and I began to argue frequently. He stayed away most of the time, but when he did show up, we would have terrible fights. It got so bad that I began to contemplate leaving him. I knew that if I were going to leave, I had to go far away because I didn't think that he would let me walk away with his child without a fight. We had a volatile relationship, and since "O" was involved in dangerous activities, I wanted to protect my child. One day after spending some time with "O" I casually told him that I was going to leave. It was a clear, sunny day, and I walked him to his car. Just before he got in his car, I told him that I was going to leave. I went on to say that this is probably the last time that he was going to see me. He looked startled but shrugged it off. He looked at me in the eyes and said: "Girl you're not going anywhere." He kissed me on my forehead, got in his car and drove off. That evening I called my brother Scott to ask him to help me drive to Georgia. I explained that I wanted to leave as soon as possible. The very next day I rented a U-Haul truck, loaded it up with the help of Scott. We arrived in Newton, Georgia eighteen hours later.

Jasmine was six months old by this time. I was so happy to see my baby girl, but it was extremely difficult for me to deal with my grandmother's verbal attacks. "Mom" had a sharp tongue and she didn't mind using it. I already felt bad enough about my failed relationship with "O" and I didn't need Mom's snide remarks. I had no idea how I was going to raise a child by myself, but I didn't have a choice. Within a few weeks, I got a job at the Albany Mall; I worked at Sears as a sales associate. I did well there, but I was miserable at home. "Mom" had a special way of making me feel inadequate, like a total failure. She and I began to argue frequently. One day we had a huge blow-up about Jasmine's father. Mom couldn't understand what I saw in "O". She thought I should just get over him and move on, which I was trying to do. But her derogatory comments and insulting statements only made me angry. Every time she said something hurtful to me about "O" I would think about her relationship with my father John Hurtman and how she ignored the signs of incest for reasons I may never understand. She was in no position to criticize or condemn me.

One day my grandmother "Mom" and I had an intense argument that almost got physical. She threatened to hit me, and I knew that if she did, I would clobber her. I really didn't want to hit my grandmother "Mom", but I felt pushed to that point. She was unrelenting and escalated the threats to the point of saying that she would cut me with the knife she had in her hand. In the heat of the moment, I called my mother Maxine, who lived in Tampa, Florida at the time. She had moved there with a man she was dating, but things weren't working out so well for them. I told my mother what was happening between "Mom" and me. I asked her if I could come stay with her for a while and she said, "Yes." All I know is that I left my grandmother as fast as I could and drove to Tampa, Florida. Jasmine was a year old; I left her in Georgia with "Mom." Even though "Mom" and I couldn't see eye-to-eye, she took extremely good care of Jasmine. My grandmother loved Jasmine as if she were her daughter, and that is how she had treated Scott - as if he was her own son. While in Tampa, I went to a business school called American

91

Business Institute during the day and worked at H. Lee Moffitt Cancer Center as a switchboard operator at night from 3 pm to 11 pm. I was a high performer on the job and in school. I was valedictorian for the program of study I undertook – Executive Secretary Plus. During this time, I visited Jasmine on weekends as often as I could. The drive from Tampa to Newton took five hours each way.

Just before graduation, my grandmother "Mom" became ill. She was so sick that she couldn't care for herself or Jasmine. I had to drop everything to see about "Mom" and to pick up Jasmine. "Mom" had a mild case of pneumonia; it was bad, but not fatal. She was definitely too weak to take care of a three-year-old. I decided to take Jasmine back to Tampa with me. Luckily, I had already completed the required course work and was just waiting for graduation day. My mother Maxine and Jasmine attended my graduation!

Once my grandmother "Mom" was well enough, I took Jasmine back to Georgia, but I had to figure out what to do with my life. Should I stay in Tampa? Should I go back to New Jersey? Moving back to Georgia wasn't an option because a big concern for me was providing a good education for Jasmine, not just in the classroom but I also wanted to expose her to a culturally diverse environment which was not available in Newton, Georgia. I talked it over with my mother and decided to move to Jersey City with a childhood friend, Kalynne. Kalynne welcomed Jasmine and me into her small apartment that she kept impeccably clean. Kalynne was intrigued by Jasmine's intellect and good manners. She lovingly referred to Jasmine as "Little Jackie." We stayed at

Kalynne's until I was able to find a full-time job, which only took me a few weeks. It wasn't long before my mother Maxine moved from Tampa to Jersey City, and we rented a condominium on Kennedy Boulevard.

I know that had I not been responsible for another human being, I would have completely self-destructed. I have often said to my daughter, Jasmine, "You saved my life."

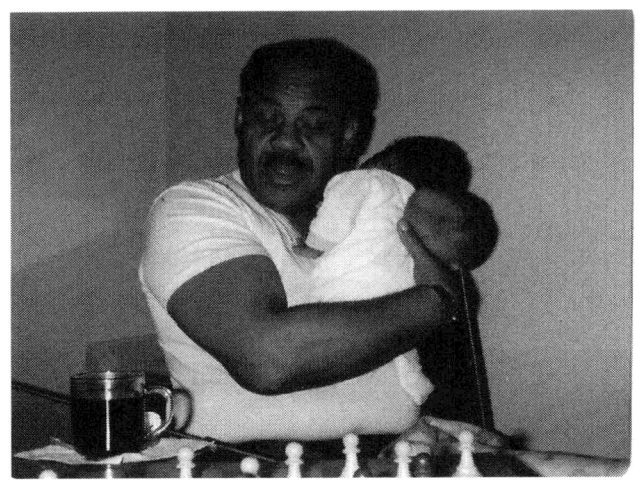

Dad and Jasmine

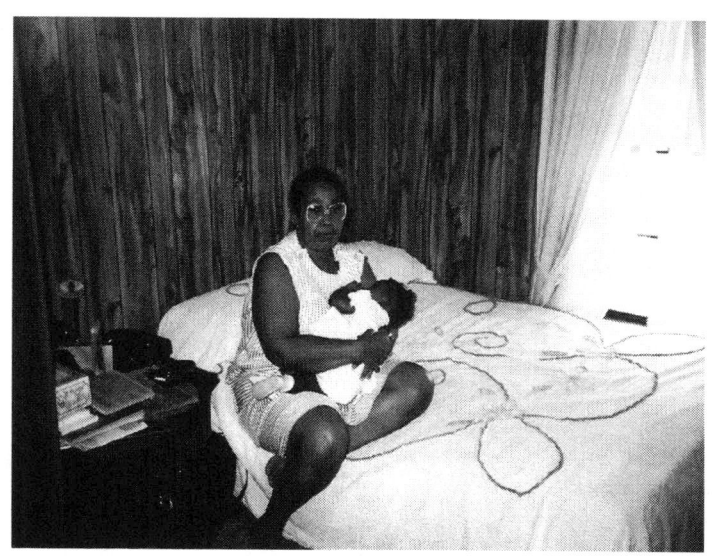

Mom and Jasmine

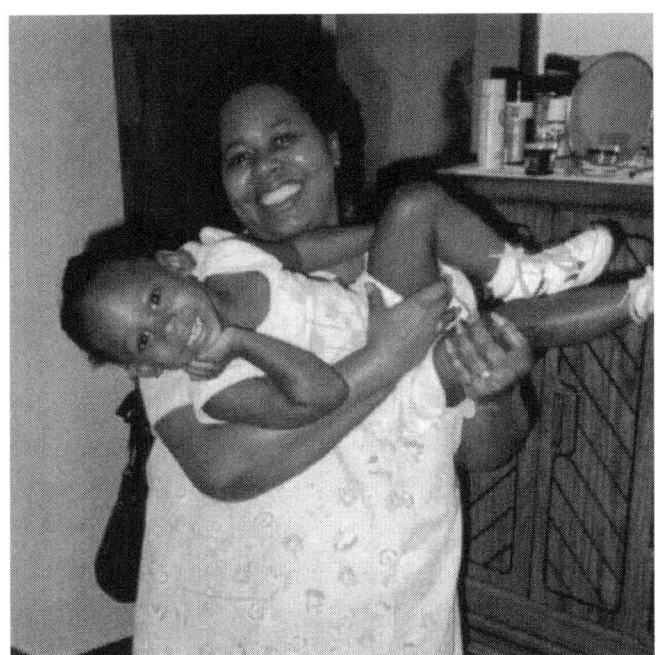

Maxine "Nana" and Jasmine

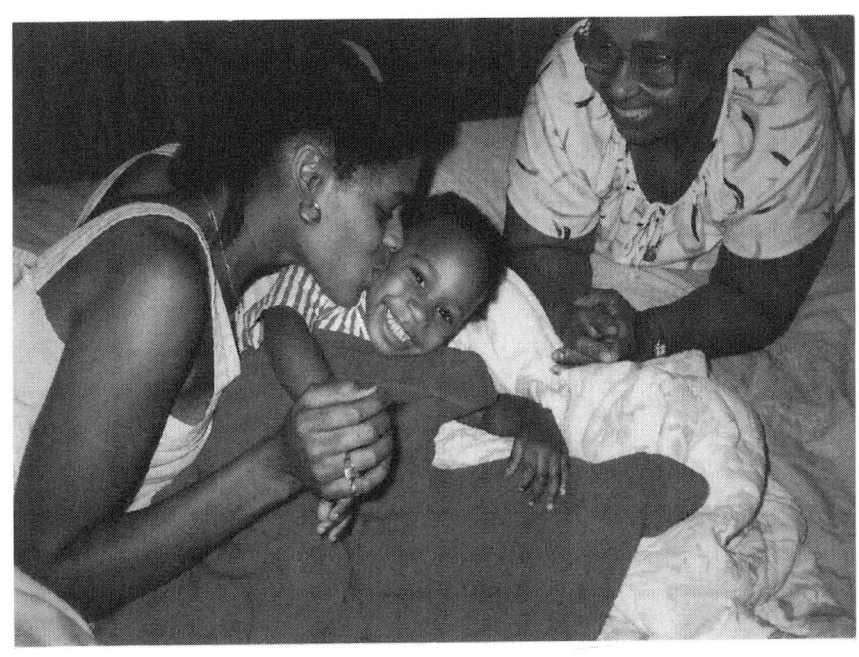

Jackie, Jasmine and Mom

> "Help your brother's boat across, and your own will reach the shore."
>
> **~ Hindu Proverb**

CHAPTER 8

Joel and Me

Marty breast-fed Joel until he was four years old. Needless to say, he had all 32 teeth by that time. I think there was something slightly incestuous about that. As soon as Joel was weaned from Marty's breast, my father took Joel and moved into a small basement apartment with Joanne on Chelten Avenue in the Germantown section of Philadelphia, not far from Abbottsford Avenue. By this time Scott was in Newark, New Jersey with me.

John, Joanne, and Joel lived on Chelten Avenue for several years but by the time Joel was seven they all moved into Joanne's old apartment on Seymour Avenue. Evidently, Joanne rented this apartment after moving in with us on Abbottsford Avenue and kept it through the years. It was a small second-floor studio apartment with a kitchen, a bathroom, and a sitting room.

Even though I had moved to Newark to live with my mother Maxine, Dad, Joel and I continued to stay in close contact. One day my father called me to ask if I would talk to my brother Joel to try to get him to finish high school and just "act right." I said, "Sure, I'll talk to Joel." It was interesting to me that on the one hand Dad wanted me to act like Joel's big sister but on the other hand he wouldn't acknowledge me as his biological daughter. I took the train to Philadelphia to visit them. My father met me at the train station, then we went to lunch. During the meal, my father explained that Joel had been giving him a hard time. I wasn't really sure what that meant but what concerned Dad the most was that Joel had been cutting school. Joel was 14 years old at the time. He attended a magnet high school for intellectually gifted students. When we finished our meal, Dad drove to Joel's school.

He said he wanted to surprise Joel. He asked me to wait in the car while he went inside the school to get Joel. I waited but my father came back to the car rather quickly, and Joel wasn't with him. When he got in the car, he said: "Joel wasn't in school today." Wow, I thought to myself, what a surprise. I really thought that Joel was the "golden child" - perfect in every way. Eventually, I did talk to my brother, but it wasn't on that day.

When Joel was sixteen years old, he began to demand answers to many questions about our family. Dad told Joel and Marty that he had done my mother Maxine a favor by taking Scott and me when we were young kids. Joel wanted the truth, and he knew that I, too, wanted to hear Dad tell us the truth about our identity. Joel had hit the peak of his rebelliousness. Not only was he skipping school but he was also hanging out late at night. Many times he didn't even come home.

One day during the summer of 1988, Joel called me and said "Jackie, let's confront Dad together. I'm sick of this bullshit, and if we confront him together, he has to tell us the truth. If he doesn't, I'll kill him!" I didn't want anybody to die, but I did want answers to the questions that plagued my life - our lives. He knew I had asked for answers --- Joel had seen me beg and plead with Dad for answers. But, Dad refused to come clean with the truth. He would always say "Jackie you can't make me say what you want me to say." My response would always be "I JUST WANT THE TRUTH!" Now Joel wanted the truth too.

I lived in Jersey City, New Jersey at the time. Joel still lived with my father and Joanne in a studio apartment on Seymour Street in the Germantown section of Philadelphia. Joel and I agreed to meet. I called Scott to tell him what we were going to do, and I drove to Philadelphia in my Hyundai. My daughter, Jasmine, was three years old. Joel and I spent the day together talking about how ridiculous his situation at home was. He told me how dad and Joanne would have sex in front of him. They all lived in one room. It was a crazy situation, and Joel was ready to explode.

Scott lived in West Philadelphia at the time. Joel and I went to Scott's apartment to tell him what our plan was. Joel had already contacted Dad, and somehow was able to get Dad to agree to meet with us to have "the talk." I think Joel threatened to kill him if he didn't meet with us. When Joel and I met with Scott, Scott said that he didn't want to get involved. He told us to go ahead without him. Joel and I were upset that Scott wouldn't come with us, but we weren't surprised because Scott usually excluded himself when it came to doing something with Joel and me. Even though my brothers love each other, there was subtle tension between them. I attribute it to the disdain Marty had for my grandmother "Mom" and vice versa. Initially, Scott was the "golden child" used as a pawn by Dad to pit Maxine against "Mom" and then "Mom" against Marty. The contest among the women/mothers was to see which male child would become the "best" man and make Dad most proud. This was never spoken in words, but it was carried out in deeds. Somehow, I became the glue that kept us together through all the chaos.

We tried to persuade Scott to come with us, but he wouldn't budge. He said something to the effect of: "You guys are going to cause me to kill somebody." I continued to beg him; I believe he wanted to join us, but there was some force that held him back. As I reflect, I guess it was for the best that he didn't go with us, because had he been there when we confronted Dad, I believe someone would have died.

It was about 8:00 p.m. or so when Joel and I left Scott's place. We drove across town to get to Dad and Joanne's apartment house. Jasmine was stretched out in the back of my car -- sound asleep. It was a hot summer night. By the time we arrived on Seymour Street, the sun had gone down completely. I parked the car in a space close to the house. As soon as we got out of the car, we saw Dad sitting on the front steps of the house. The porch light was shining brightly. He had earplugs in his ears and a Walkman in his hand. It was very unusual for my father to be listening to a Walkman and I had no idea what he was listening to, but I would imagine it was something inspirational to prepare him for what was about to happen. Did I mention that Joel had a 32-pistol tucked in the waist of his pants? Well he did, and it was concealed under his shirt. Just in case things got out of hand, I had a knife in my oversized pocketbook. Dad was going to have to answer our questions, willingly or unwillingly. We were ready!

As we approached the steps, Dad took out the earplugs. We greeted one another. Dad asked us if we wanted to go inside and Joel said: "No, let's stay out here on the porch." Dad grabbed the banister and got up

101

slowly. He said okay, and we walked toward the center of the porch. I led the conversation because Joel was really angry. He maintained his composure, but I knew he was ready to fire off on Dad. I'm sure Dad knew it too. I said, "Dad you know why we're here. We want to know the truth. Are you Scott's and my father? And is Maxine our mother?" Dad paused and started to say something about it being a complicated situation. "What do you mean complicated?" I retorted. "Either you're our father, or you're not!"

Admitting to being our father meant that Dad would have to admit to having an incestuous relationship with Maxine. It would also mean that he would have to confess the truth to Joel, his "golden child" who was given preferential treatment by him. Joel sat on the front banister, with one leg lifted and the other foot planted firmly, a few feet from us. Dad and I were now standing near the front door. Dad was right where we wanted him – cornered. It felt like he was about to confess. Then all of a sudden Joanne opened the front door. "What's going on? John, what's going on?" Dad told Joanne to go back inside. But Joanne insisted on knowing what we were talking about. I said this doesn't concern you, Joanne. Joel didn't budge, and he didn't say a word. Joanne then said: "Anything that concerns your father concerns me." I said "REALLY?! Well does this concern you?" Before I knew it, I had grabbed Joanne by the collar; I started punching her in her face. I knocked her glasses off. My father reached for me; he tried to hold me. I shook him off, and one of my punches caught his chin. Joanne yelled out for help. She said something about calling the cops. I continued to beat her down and said, "You've gotta get to a phone first, Joanne." I kept punching her. With all the strength in my body, I punched and pounded on her back. My father had backed off and let Joanne take the punches. Joel finally grabbed me when he saw that I had started to reach for my purse, where I had hidden the knife. I stopped throwing punches, picked up my bag, gathered my composure, and looked at my father and Joanne square in their eyes. Joanne was beet-red, and her clothes were disheveled, then Joel and I walked down the steps and headed towards my car. In all this commotion, Jasmine was still sound asleep. We called Scott to tell him what had just happened. The sad thing was that we didn't have any more information than we had prior to meeting with Dad.

The following day I called Maxine, "Mom" and Marty to tell them what had happened. Each one was surprised, but they all seemed to be glad that I had the courage to confront John Hurtman; something they never did. Not one of them felt bad for Joanne. Joel did not stay another night at the apartment with Dad and Joanne after this incident. The following week he took all his belongings including his 5-foot long boa constrictor. Three months after that Dad and Joanne were married!

Joel got caught-up in the street. He became a hustler, made fast money, and then tried to clean up his act. Despite the issues between Joel and Dad, they stayed in touch. With the help and guidance of Dad, Joel learned to be a shrewd businessman. For a time, my father managed a pretzel shop for Joel, which meant that they still saw each other on a regular basis. Joel also had three beeper stores, one of them in the Germantown area of Philadelphia, which consumed most of his time. Before long, Joel purchased several properties and created a real estate business that became a success. By the time Joel turned thirty, he was a millionaire.

Joel became a father at age eighteen; his son and daughter are nine months apart by different women. If Joel had a weakness, it was sex. Joel hated his mother, Marty, until the day she died on February 13, 2013. Even now when he talks about Marty he refers to her as "a piece of shit."

On January 30, 2016, Joel and I had a conversation via text, which is below in its entirety.

Joel --

Was reading this and thought of you, "traits of a sociopath: Superficial charm Manipulative, shallow emotions, lack of shame or guilt no matter what they have done, need for stimulation: gambling, promiscuity and being extremely religious are common. Lack of empathy, impulsive nature, law abiding, unreliability, infidelity and unusual sexuality, conventional appearance, seeks to control or enslavement of others especially who they see as weaker or less intelligent, likes to be around those who they can be superior over, very high IQ, threatened by those they see as more intelligent or stronger than them. Will give money or gifts to those they see they can manipulate. Cares little for their actions/affect on others, callous to others crying or emotions. Rationalizes pain they inflict on others, mental problems usually with onset by 15, poor work behavior but often able to be wealthy, willing to abuse their own children if it fits their agenda, doesn't think they have done anything wrong."

Is this not Marty 101? Is there anything on the list that doesn't fit and speak to the disease she was? Anyway, how are you?

Me --

sounds like dad

Except for the money part because he never had enough money to really help anybody out financially

Joel --

Marty had way more of the list than dad, but dad had many as well

Me --

Marty learned from the best Joel

Joel --

(1/6) Marty fooled more people than dad, though; she still has u, and Scott fooled. Dad probably was one as well; he wasn't as impulsive and certainly never made

(2/6) any money, he didn't have diagnosed mental problems at 15 like Marty. A huge difference is dad had nothing; he was abused as a child; Marty had everything

(3/6) given to her. Dad wanted good for his children, he just couldn't get out of his own way, and had an ego that didn't match

his ability. Marty didn't give

(4/6) a shit about her child that she felt she couldn't manipulate, she gravitated to those she felt she could, which is a trait of sociopaths. Had her church

(5/6) said she needed to kill me, she would have done it in a heartbeat. She only cared for her agenda; she cared nothing for me. For all his bullshit, Dad wasn't.'

(6/6) like that.

Me --

Dad destroyed every woman who loved him and did significant damage to his children.

You give dad a huge pass and blame Marty for everything. I wish you had met Marty before she got hooked up in that religion. Dad was a pedophile long before Marty came on the scene.

Why do you refuse to see that?

Joel --

(1/6) I don't give dad a pass. He was fucked up. I know he was a molester. He was also abused. Marty had more resources, though, a pampered life and overall she

(2/6) was every bit as fucked up as he was. He couldn't have done all he did without her. She had the world given to her, and she did nothing for her child. And

(3/6) til the end she blamed me for it all, as a sociopath does.

While dad couldn't admit it in public, I saw things that said to me he was remorseful to some

(4/6) extent, Marty wasn't, she remained the piece of shit she was til the end, and in her writings and what she said to me in death, she was a spiteful bitch.

(5/6) Maybe I did hate her, which is much more than she deserves. I am just being real based on the facts. You don't see it all, and I realize u don't have

(6/6) the benefit of the information that I have. But this is the reality of it all

Me --

You have every right to be angry. It's a fucked up situation, and we had fucked up parents. All things considered, I'm proud of you Scott and myself. We have changed the game and for that I am eternally grateful!!!

Dad was more than a molester. He had two children with his stepdaughter. And then denied that he was the father. He held that lie until the day he died.

Maybe you had the benefit of seeing signs of remorse from him, but Scott and I didn't.

End of a text conversation.

When I left Philadelphia in 1972 things fell apart back home. Joel was still a baby and my older brother, Scott, was 12 years old. Scott thought that with me gone he would get more attention; being the oldest of the children I guess he felt slighted in some ways. However, the exact opposite happened. Soon after I left Philadelphia, Marty began taking an interest in Jehovah's Witness. People would come by for Bible study sessions with Marty on a frequent basis; she converted and became a Jehovah's Witness. Once that happened, she was a changed person. Scott told me that when Marty converted to Jehovah's Witness, she began to ignore him; her sole focus was on Joel and religion. Scott stayed in Philadelphia as long as he could but ultimately he left Philadelphia and came to Newark where I was living.

Religion gave Marty the courage to stand up to my father in ways that she couldn't do on her own. She now had the Bible as a point of reference to guide her life, and she had the backing of her religious community to support her in the actions that she decided to take. Marty made it clear that she was no longer going to participate in an adulterous relationship. Unfortunately, my father was successful in taking Joel from her. I believe that Marty had a nervous breakdown, but she was never medically treated as such. It was apparent that when my father took Joel, she was virtually destroyed. Marty immersed herself in religious studies. Periodically Marty would send religious pamphlets to me. The only communication I had with her during this time was via postal service mail. From time to time, she would send me a Watch Tower magazine along with a note encouraging me to convert to the only true religion, Jehovah's Witness.

To this day, Joel has a deep resentment toward Marty for abandoning him. He feels that his mother chose religion over him. To me, on the surface, it is true; she chose the Jehovah's Witness religion over her only son. But, I also think that had it not been for religion, Marty would have been institutionalized, or she would have died an early death. Marty sacrificed everything she knew in order to have a relationship with John Hurtman. Her extended family became estranged because of it. Her childhood friends disassociated themselves from her. And, many people questioned her relationship with my father and her willingness to take care of his two black children.

My father told Marty that Scott and I were not his biological children and that he was doing Maxine a favor by caring for us. Marty believed what he told her. As the years went by, she maintained a less contentious relationship with Scott and me than she did with Joel. Based on the many conversations that I have had with my brothers about Marty, it is evident that the woman who raised Scott and me was very different from the woman who gave birth to my brother Joel. Joel never saw Marty as the vibrant, charismatic, intelligent woman that Scott and I got to see. By the time he came into the world, Marty was a broken woman. All her dreams of a happy family had dissolved. She took a huge chance with my father. The love that Marty once poured into my father she learned to pour into religion. Ultimately, she devoted her entire life to her ministry within the Jehovah's Witness religious community. The "believers" within the religious community were the only people with whom Marty would associate. The only conversations that Marty would engage in were religiously focused.

Joel reached out to Marty on several occasions during his pre-teen years hoping that she would help him or rescue him from the hell he was experiencing living with Dad and Joanne. Marty told him that the only way she would agree to help was under the condition that he convert to her religion, which Joel refused to do. Marty enabled John Hurtman and put a condition on Joel to accept religion in order for her to protect him. Marty failed her son Joel and used religion as the excuse. As a result, Joel blamed Marty for everything that went wrong during his childhood and did not accept that Marty was another victim of Dad's abusive behavior. Joel hates religion and does not believe in God. For a while he proclaimed to be agnostic, but since the death of his mother he now professes to be an atheist. If he hates anything more than his mother Marty, I would have to say it is religion. Joel has often declared: "Money is my god!"

Dad and Baby Joel

Marty and Joel

Marty, Jackie and Joel

Jackie and Joel

Jackie and Joel

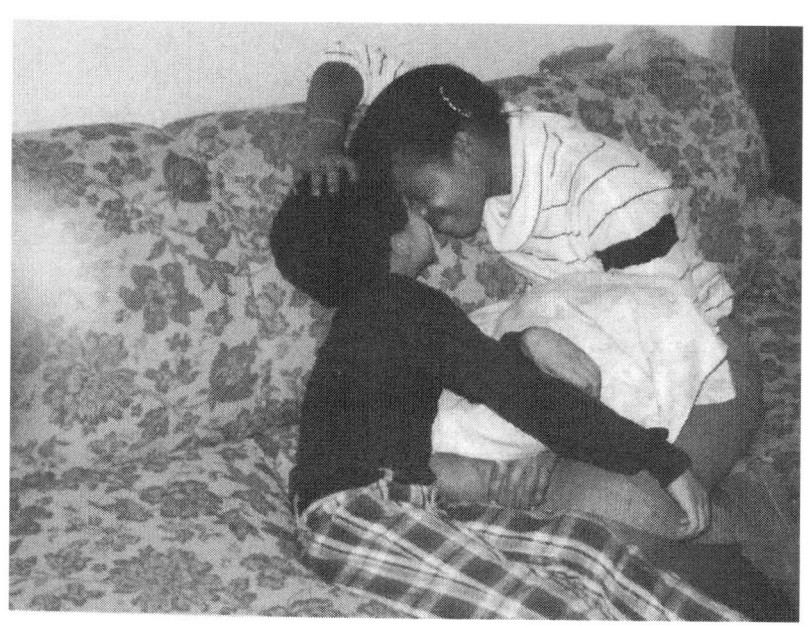

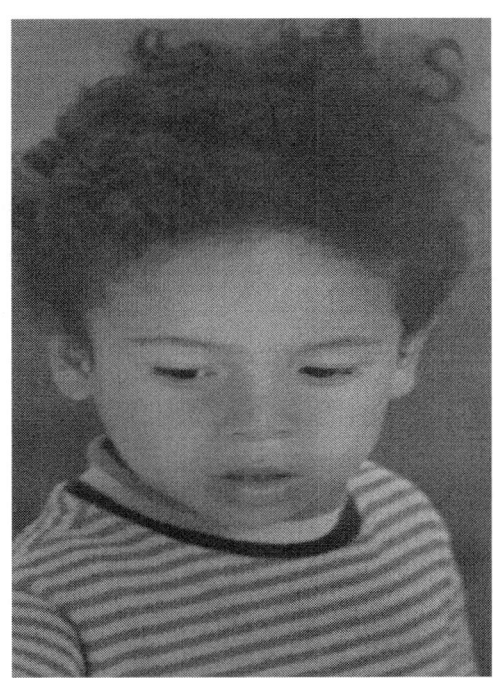

Joel age 5

"You can come out of the furnace of trouble two ways: if you let it consume you, you come out a cinder; but there is a kind of metal which refuses to be consumed, and comes out a star."

~ *Jean Church, Overcoming Addiction*

CHAPTER 9

Addiction

When I was thirteen years old, I tried marijuana for the first time. I remember it like it was yesterday. An Italian girl in my eighth grade class gave me a joint and said, "Come on try this!" So I did. I tried cocaine when I was fifteen, and I was nineteen years old when I started smoking cigarettes. The crew "O" ran with did cocaine and heroin on a regular basis, so eventually I followed along and tried it. I tried free-basing once or twice by the time I was twenty. Cocaine/free-basing became my drug of choice. When I was high, I was able to talk about my family story. Believe it or not, it was during my episodes of getting high that I started to put the pieces of my crazy life together.

By some miracle of God when I became pregnant with Jasmine, I did not smoke cigarettes or use drugs. Several months after I graduated from business school, I got Jasmine from my grandmother "Mom" and moved to Jersey City, New Jersey. Soon after we arrived, I enrolled Jasmine in pre-school; she was the smartest child in the group. By age three Jasmine was reading. Not only was Jasmine smart, but she was also well mannered and highly inquisitive. It didn't take long for me to find a job as an Administrative Assistant at Rockefeller Center in New York City. I worked for a construction company; the office suite was located on Fifth Avenue. I loved the job, the people, and the location. My mother was hired at a bank also in New York City, and we were getting along. We were acting like everything was okay, but all the issues of my childhood were still unresolved. I still didn't know for sure who my father was. Even though I was in touch with John Hurtman, the man I thought to be my father, he wouldn't admit it. He would just say things like: "I love you as if you were my daughter, Jackie." My brother Scott was traveling the world as a fitness trainer. He was in Europe at this time. Joel was a troubled teenager, grappling with many of the same issues that I was. My mother Maxine just didn't want to talk about it. In her mind, some things were better left unsaid. In my mind, **SOME THINGS _MUST_ BE SAID!**

As fate would have it, I met a drug dealer when I lived in Jersey City; my mother Maxine moved into the basement apartment with Jasmine and me, which was located on Kennedy Boulevard. The drug dealer sold me the line that I didn't have to spend any money; he just wanted to get to know me better. He had cocaine, and he knew how to cook-it-up to free-base. So I bought the line and said "yes." He came to my apartment late one night; it was close to midnight when he arrived. We sat in the living room, talked and smoked. The bedroom doors to my room and my mother's room were closed but to this day, I believe that my mother knew what I was doing. It was the same old pattern of behavior.

Eventually, my mother left my place and moved to a studio apartment in Irvington, New Jersey. It wasn't long after that that I was laid-off. The construction company I worked for went out of business. I was devastated. Jasmine attended Catholic School, so I had tuition to pay, rent to pay, and a car note. It was a really low time in my life. Unemployment was not enough to meet my financial obligations. I ended up moving to Irvington into the small studio apartment with my mother.

Jasmine was five years old now. Since I was unemployed, I decided to go back to school. I got through one semester at Rutgers University in Newark, and then I found a clerical job. The feelings of mental and emotional confusion continued. My mother knew that I wanted answers, but she acted like everything was all right. Whenever the conversation about my identity would come up, my mother would clam-up.

It wasn't long after moving into the studio apartment with my mother, that someone I had met through a college acquaintance introduced me to another drug dealer, who lived in the building adjacent to ours. This man let me know right away that he wanted to have me around. On one occasion, no sooner than we entered his apartment and sat down, he offered me a rock of cocaine, put it in a pipe, fired it up, and passed the glass genie to me. Oh, what a feeling! The "high" hit like a wave of cool water. It took all the pain away, at least for the moment. We stayed up for a while, smoking and talking. I didn't talk much but I did listen to the small talk between the men that were in the apartment. Amazingly, I managed to keep an eye on the time because Jasmine was at home with my mother, and I knew that I had to be home before she woke up. My mother didn't seem to care what I did. She didn't question me about where I was or what I had been doing. When I got home, I tiptoed to the bathroom to get ready for bed and then climbed on the top bunk bed to sleep off the high. Jasmine was sound asleep on the lower bunk, and my mother was asleep in a full-sized bed next to the bunk beds. Later that morning when Jasmine and my mother woke up, I acted like everything was okay.

As time passed, I started getting high more regularly. I looked forward to the weekend because that became my routine – Friday and Saturday nights I would sneak out late at night to get high. As I smoked, I tried to make sense of all the things that were troubling me or I simply tried to forget about them. Consistent with my out-of-control life was the out-of-control debt that I had accumulated. I had credit card debt and was barely making it from paycheck to paycheck. I contemplated suicide and even told my mother that I was ready to die. One day when I was at home alone, I turned on the gas stove and hoped to suffocate from the gas fumes. I called my mother Maxine to let her know, but she seemed very calm about it. I don't remember exactly what she said, but it basically amounted to -- go ahead and kill yourself if that's what you want to do. I was too much of a coward to kill myself, and I knew that if I died it would have a horrible effect on Jasmine. I turned the gas off and decided to live another day. It just felt like the pressure of the world was closing in on me. My Hyundai was re-possessed. I lied and told everybody who asked that the car was stolen. My mother went along with the story. Just lies, lies, and more lies...

I kept hoping and praying that somehow things would get better. Even after an episode of getting high, I would pray to God for forgiveness and for the desire to get high to be taken away from me. I would cry and pray, and pray and cry. I wanted a better life for Jasmine and for me, but mostly for Jasmine. She deserved so much better. I finally got the nerve to make an appointment with Essex Legal Services, an agency that provides free legal counsel to low-income residents in Essex County, New

Jersey. Prior to my appointment, I gathered my bills and put together all of the information I was told that I would need for the consultation with the attorney. I arrived early for the appointment, signed in, and waited patiently in the reception area for my name to be called. When my name was finally called, I was met by a tall, handsome man who happened to be the attorney. He introduced himself, Attorney Calvinton Louis – "Calvin", and led the way to his office. Once seated, I explained my financial situation to him. He was very pleasant and discussed with me the various options available to address my debt. He gave me his card, told me to think things through, and to let him know what my decision would be.

When I met with the attorney, not only did I bring a large envelope that contained my credit card statements but I also brought a notebook to jot down important details during my conversation with him. In the same book, I had notes previously written about my fitness and financial goals, among other things. To my surprise, later in the day after meeting with attorney Louis, he called me to tell me that I left my notebook in his office. He said he would hold on to it until I was able to come back to get it. I said that I would come the following day. We agreed that I should come in the afternoon.

When I arrived, I was escorted to his office. I had on a pair of freshly starched blue jeans, a crisp white polo shirt, and white sneakers. My hair was neatly pulled back into a ponytail. As soon as I entered his office, I thanked him for returning the notebook to me, at which time he began a conversation about physical fitness. He had obviously read some of the entries I had made in the notebook, but I didn't think much of it. We continued to talk for a short time, and then I left.

The next day he called me at home and asked me out on a dinner date. I didn't think it was appropriate for him to ask a client to go out on a date but I told him that I would think about it and get back to him and if that was all right. He said: "Okay." I thought about it for a few days and then said: "Yes. I'll go out to dinner with you." We had a nice time together. That was the beginning of our courtship. I was still getting high from time to time, but I didn't tell Calvin until one day I had been getting high, and I wanted more. When the "free" cocaine was all gone, I used my money to buy a few rocks of cooked cocaine. I brought them to my mother's studio apartment. My mother wasn't there, but Jasmine was. I went into the bathroom and rigged-up an empty soda bottle so that I could smoke the rocks. I had been in the bathroom for quite some time when Jasmine knocked on the door and said that she had to go to the bathroom. Jasmine was seven years old.

I didn't want her to come in the bathroom because it was full of smoke. I opened the door; I'm sure I looked crazy – glassy eyes – sweaty brow – totally out of my mind. I grabbed a bucket that was right outside the bathroom door. I told Jasmine to pee in the bucket. I went back into the bathroom, closed the door, and continued smoking. When I smoked the last rock, I cleaned the bathroom. I took a quick bath and then came out. That was my lowest point!!! How could I shut my daughter out of the bathroom and allow her to piss in a pail?! How could I be so out-of-control to smoke while my daughter stood right outside the bathroom door?! How could I do this to my very own flesh and blood?!

I was completely out of my mind. I told Jasmine that I wanted to leave – move to another city or state. I told her that I had to take care of some business, and I'd be right back. I left her at home alone. I walked to Irvington Center to the Investors Savings Bank to withdraw the money I had in my savings account. It wasn't much, but it was enough to pay for a motel room. When I left the bank, I walked to the Irvington Motor Inn to rent a room. The room was dark and dirty just like my mental state. As soon as I walked into the room, I called Calvin. I told him that I had been doing drugs, and I needed help. I felt so bad I wanted to die. I just wanted to end it all and DIE! Calvin wanted to come get me right away, but I told him not to. I stayed at the motel by myself for an hour or so. I remember holding my face in my hands and crying my heart out. I cried and cried. I asked God to help me; please forgive me and protect my child: "God, please look past my faults and bless my child. This isn't her fault." I don't actually remember how long I was there, but I know that I didn't spend the night and the sun was still shining when I walked back to the apartment building. Somehow, I got myself together and walked home.

When I returned to the apartment building, as soon as I opened the door to the lobby, I saw Jasmine. She was worried about me. She hugged me and asked me where I had been. Our apartment was on the fourth floor; I didn't want to use the elevator, so we took the stairs. Jasmine asked me a million questions: "Where were you, Mommy? Are you all right? What's wrong?"

I said, "Mommy is sick, and she needs help." "What's wrong Mommy what's the matter?" "I'm going to be okay Jasmine. I just need some help. I promise you I'm going to be all right." I apologized to Jasmine for leaving her alone and for asking her to urinate in a pail. **THAT WAS THE WORST DAY OF MY ADULT LIFE!**

<u>Recovery Begins</u>

I called around to find out how to get drug treatment. Luckily, I had insurance. I called an 800 number to ask for help and got connected to a drug treatment facility in Summit, New Jersey. Calvin said he would drive me there.

When my mother Maxine came home, I told her what had happened. By this time, I had already made arrangements to be evaluated for admission into the drug rehabilitation program. I was advised to participate in an intensive outpatient program. At that point, I would have done anything to stop using drugs. I wanted somebody to teach me how to cope with everything that had happened in my life. I desperately wanted to be a good mother to Jasmine, and I was not only destroying my life but had also placed Jasmine's life in danger as well. Jasmine was so bright, so intelligent, so beautiful, and so important to me. I had to get myself together. I really didn't know what to do; I didn't know if drug treatment was going to work and I felt so helpless. The pain I felt was deep down on the inside of my being. Except for Jasmine, everything about my life seemed meaningless, and I knew that I had to get myself together for her.

I called my grandmother "Mom" to ask her if I could bring Jasmine to Georgia to live with her until I got the help I needed for my drug problem. She said yes. Everything was happening so fast. I pulled Jasmine out of school. I came up with a story for her fourth-grade teacher. My grandmother enrolled Jasmine in school at Baker County Elementary School in Newton, Georgia. I began treatment immediately. I went to a Alcoholics Anonymous or Narcotics Anonymous group meeting every day. I was tested for drugs and alcohol on a weekly basis and began to learn what it means to live life one day at a time – to accept life on life's terms.

In addition to group sessions, I agreed to meet with a psychologist on a bi-weekly basis. I told my therapist Angela what led me to seek help and how I was referred to her. I shared that I wanted to learn how to cope with the issues of my life. She asked me what my "issues" were so I told her about my family, the incest, my abortions, how my mother Maxine changed my name, the lies, and the secrets. I told her I had to learn to cope, or I was going to die. But, I couldn't die because I had to live for Jasmine.

When I told Angela my story, even her jaw dropped. The fact that a psychology professional was shocked by my story further confirmed that I was dealing with a very strange set of circumstances. I mean really, what kind of people do these kinds of things – impregnate your step-daughter not once but twice -- take the children – have them call you daddy, but then change the story mid-stream – tell the children that they have different mothers and different fathers – and to top it all off – their fathers are dead – perpetuate the cycle of sexual abuse by not believing your child when she tells you that your fiancé has been sexually abusing her – call her a jealous liar – change her name to that of her abuser without even having a discussion about it – make her abort her unborn children without having a discussion about it – change her schools every two years – ship her off to Georgia during her last year of high school because the abusive step-father is terminally ill with cancer – and simply refuse to tell the truth because the lie became the truth.

After seeing Angela for a few months, she told me that it would be a good idea to have my mother Maxine come with me to my next session. I thought that might be helpful too; but, when I mentioned it to my mother she said "Oh no. You might need therapy, but I'm not going." I said, "But the doctor said it would be beneficial for me to have you come with me since I've talked to her about you and the family." My mother said, "No, I'm not going to do it." I was hurt and deeply disappointed.

When I showed up for my next session without my mother Maxine, Angela didn't seem surprised. She asked me what happened, and I told her what my mother said. Angela then said, "Jackie, I really didn't think your mother would show up for you, but I needed you to see that. She had never shown up for you when it really mattered, and yet you've managed to handle whatever has come your way." My response was "WOW! You're right! Maybe I'm stronger than I think I am." That was my light bulb moment, my epiphany! I'd been coping all along. In my mind, I was failing. I felt that everybody could tell that I was confused, abused, and living a lie. I felt inferior, inadequate, unimportant, insignificant – TOTALLY INVISIBLE. From that moment forward, I began to see myself differently. I began to see my strength, my courage, and my goodness.

By the end of the summer of 1994, I was ready to get Jasmine from my grandmother. I drove to Georgia by myself. I stayed in Georgia only long enough to pack up all of Jasmine's belongings and to get a little rest before the drive back to New Jersey. My grandmother "Mom" seemed to enjoy having Jasmine with her for a few months. I was happy to be taking her home with me. Once we loaded up the car and said our "good-byes" we headed for Interstate 95-North. Jasmine told me all about her stay with "Mom." She talked about the school she attended and the friends she had made.

I shared openly and honestly about my illness. When I took Jasmine to my grandmother's house, I had told her that I was sick. I didn't go into detail about it, but I tried to assure her as best I could that I would be all right. I felt it was my duty to explain to Jasmine what my illness was. This was one of the toughest yet most important conversations that I've ever had with my daughter. I explained how hurt and confused I had felt through the years because of lies and misinformation I was given about my identity. I told her that I used drugs as a means to numb the pain, but it only made things worse. I repeatedly said: "None of this is your fault, Jasmine." I went on to say, "Jasmine, I want you to know the truth, and I want you to know that I love you dearly. Mommy just has to learn to cope with all that has transpired. I apologize for what I did, Jasmine. You deserve so much better, and I promise to do better. No matter where I am or what I'm going through I promise that we will go through it together." I cried as I shared the truth with Jasmine while I tried to keep my eyes on the road. I told Jasmine that people in the family might tell her that Scott isn't my brother, but I'm telling you the truth. Scott is my brother and John Hurtman "Poppy" is our father. The few times that Jasmine saw my father she referred to him as "Poppy." Yes, he was married to "Mom" but he had sex with my mother Maxine (who Jasmine called Nana) and impregnated her two times. They don't want the truth to be told, but I'm telling it. "And, Jasmine, if you don't, believe me, I encourage you to check into it for yourself. Another source of my pain is the fact that the man Nana married sexually abused me and when I told Nana about it, she said I was lying to her. She even changed my last name to his, even after I had told her what he did to me. So, Jasmine, that's why I have always told you that you have to guard your personal space. No one should ever touch you unless you want to be touched. If anyone ever violates you by touching your private parts, please tell me right away. If for some reason I don't respond the way you want me to, then tell me until you get satisfaction. Promise me that you'll do it." Jasmine responded, "I promise."

Calvin

Just before I went to Georgia to get Jasmine, Calvin and I decided to get an apartment together. We rented a two-bedroom apartment in Sayreville, New Jersey. Just prior to leaving to get Jasmine, we went out to dinner. During

127

our conversation over dinner, I told Calvin in a matter-of-fact way, "I have enough love for you and Jasmine. The love for a man is different from the love for a child." I went on to say, "I just want you to know that if you ever touch my child in an inappropriate manner, I will chop your dick off." Calvin was stunned by what I said and quickly responded by asking, "Why would you say something like that to me, Jackie?" Without hesitation, I said, "I just want you to know that there will be consequences if you touch my child inappropriately. I'll go to hell or jail for my child. If anything should happen, you've been put on notice." I didn't raise my voice and neither did he. He then said that he couldn't believe I would say something like that to him. I told him that I just need him to know up front. The conversation moved on to something else, but I had made myself clear.

When Jasmine and I arrived at the Winding Woods Apartment Complex in Sayreville, New Jersey, Calvin came outside to help carry Jasmine's belongings into the apartment. I had set up Jasmine's room for her. I wanted her to be as comfortable as possible, especially considering all that she had been through. She seemed to like her room and was glad to be with me. But that very first night in the apartment, Calvin attacked me. He choked me until I had to scream. Jasmine came running into our bedroom, which was across the hall from hers. She yelled out: "Stop hitting my mommy!" Calvin finally stopped. As soon as he released his grip, I walked toward Jasmine, gently placed my hands on her shoulders and asked her to go back to her room for a few minutes. I told her that I would be there shortly. I closed the bedroom door grabbed the telephone and smashed it into Calvin's face. I told him "You better never put your hands on me again!" Calvin grabbed his face, but he didn't come after me or try to hit me back. I went straight to Jasmine's room, called my mother Maxine to tell her what just happened. I asked her if we could come to her apartment and she said okay. I then called Calvin's father, hoping that he would talk sense to his son but he didn't do anything about it. I also called Jasmine's father hoping that he would show up to support Jasmine during this challenging time. He refused. He did not support Jasmine at all. He wouldn't spend time with her, and he didn't provide financial support. He didn't keep his promise to always to take care of his daughter. All I could think is here we go again... MORE DRAMA! The difference was I had made a commitment to face life on life's terms **drug-free**. I was still in recovery, receiving outpatient therapy, and Calvin had agreed to support me through the process. So, why would he act this way?

I explained to my psychologist what had happened, and she said that she wanted to meet him to talk about the situation. For my next appointment, I brought Calvin and Jasmine with me. During the counseling session, Calvin disclosed the reason for attacking me. He said that he found a journal of mine that was tucked away. In the journal, I had written about my drug use. He thought that I had had sex with the guy who gave me drugs. Instead of talking to me about it, he assumed the worst. First of all, he shouldn't have read my journal without my permission. It was a violation of privacy. Regardless of what he read, it was no excuse for the physical abuse.

Even though Calvin apologized for his actions, I still wasn't convinced that he was sincere.

We had a period of separation but eventually Calvin asked me to marry him. Our tumultuous relationship continued, and so did Calvin's jealousy. I remained committed to him and was a good girlfriend and fiancée. I wanted to open up and share my true self, but I didn't realize at the time that he wasn't interested in really knowing me. He fell in love with my body. Calvin wanted sex! Period! I made the mistake of sharing some of my story with him, which he couldn't handle. After sharing some information about my past with him, he became enraged and stormed off. It was as if I had shattered his fantasy.

A few months after that, Calvin's brother died of AIDS, which sent him into a fit of depression. His brother had lived at home with his mother prior to dying. Calvin was concerned about his mom living alone, so I made the suggestion to have her come stay with us. Within weeks, Calvin's mom was living with us. Even though his mom had been diagnosed with dementia, I really thought that I could love her back to her "sane" self. After his mom had moved in, Calvin was upset most of the time. Taking care of a sick, elderly person requires a great deal of patience, which Calvin did not possess. The more I tried to make everything seem "normal" the worse things got. Jasmine, wise beyond her young age, told me that I was way too nice to Calvin and his mom, especially since Calvin was disgruntled most of the time.

It became evident that we needed more space, and Calvin agreed to hire a realtor to help us look for a new home. We had found a few houses that I thought were suitable, but Calvin was reluctant to commit. Finally, we got to a point where I thought we had mutually decided to make an offer for a house in Maplewood, New Jersey. I was excited and hopeful; but every time I asked Calvin about it, he made up an excuse as to why he hadn't heard from the realtor. Frustration set in, so I called the realtor myself only to find out that Calvin hadn't put down a deposit, and the process wasn't moving forward. When I asked Calvin about it, he became very angry and incited an argument, which led to us both saying harsh words. Ultimately, he said that he was going to move his mother back to her house in Montclair, and he was going to leave as well.

I was definitely not expecting him to say that! "Okay, so if you're going to leave, then Jasmine and I will stay in the apartment until we can find somewhere else to live." He said, "No. This apartment is in my name, and when I go, you and Jasmine have to leave." "Really Calvin?! At least, give me some time to find another apartment." He refused. The next morning as we were driving to work together in his car, we continued the conversation, only we were a bit more civil towards each other. Unfortunately, Calvin held to his position regarding the matter, which left me feeling angry, confused, and vindictive. I asked Calvin if he was sure about leaving. He said, "Yes!" I responded by saying, "Well, keep in mind that all is fair in love and war." He said, "Whatever!" in a sarcastic tone. We rode the rest of the way in silence.

As soon as I got to my desk at work I called my mother, Maxine. I explained to her what was happening.

I was devastated, but I knew that I had to take quick action because I could not allow Calvin to put my daughter or me in the street. After speaking with my mother, I called my brother Joel to ask him a huge favor. He said, "Sure, whatever you need just let me know." I told Joel to give me a few days to pack up my things and set everything up so that all he had to do was move all my stuff onto a truck and take it to my mother's apartment. Unbeknownst to Calvin, every day after work I was packing boxes and placing them in the closets. He had gotten into the habit of coming home to our apartment pretty late, which gave me all the time I needed to pack. By mid-week, I had everything ready to go. I had already transferred Jasmine to a school in Maplewood because I really thought that we were going to move into the beautiful house there. In the morning when I dropped Jasmine off at school I explained to her that we were going to leave the Sayreville apartment. I told her that Uncle Joel was going to move all of our belongings for us, and we were going to move in with Nana (my mother). Jasmine did not seem troubled by this news.

As soon as I got to work, I called my mother and Joel. My mother came to my job to get the keys to my car and to the apartment. She drove to the Sayreville apartment to wait for Joel. I let Joel know that my mother would be waiting for him to arrive and she knew where everything was that needed to be moved. The plan was in effect. When my mother got to the apartment, she called to let me know. It wasn't long after that that Joel and four of his friends showed up to get the job done. I gave instructions to move everything that belonged to me but to leave everything of Calvin's behind. Everything except the living room furniture was mine, so the apartment was left virtually empty. Just prior to the end of my workday, Calvin called me to ask if I would meet him in his office. I agreed to meet him immediately after work. When I arrived, he was pleasant and asked if we could work things out. I was very surprised that he had softened his tone, but it was too late; my plan was already in motion. I remained poised in order not to give away the plan. At the end of our meeting, we hugged, and he said that he would see me at the apartment. I then went straight to my mother's apartment who had already picked up Jasmine from school. We laughed and joked about the situation. I was truly grateful to have gotten away from Calvin without incident.

The next day my mother kept my car and drove Jasmine to school and then dropped me off at work. It was scary because we all knew that Calvin had an explosive temper. However, what happened next caught me completely off guard. I was sitting at my desk when Calvin showed up at my job with a police officer. The police officer approached my desk, asked me if I was Jacquelin Chavez. I said, "Yes." He asked me if there was a private room where we could talk. I pointed to the small room that we used as a lunchroom. Calvin led the way; the police officer and I followed. Once inside the room, Calvin accused me of stealing his furniture. I explained to the officer in a calm voice what had happened. I was trying to speak softly because I didn't want everyone in my department to know what was going on. I told the officer that we were experiencing problems in our relationship, and Calvin planned to leave. I had asked for time to find a place to live, but Calvin was adamant about me vacating the apartment. Yes, I left without telling Calvin, but everything I packed belonged to me. Calvin was fuming; his light brown face had nearly turned completely red. Luckily for me, the Essex County police officer from the county where I worked had no jurisdiction over Middlesex County, the county where the apartment was located. He told Calvin that he would have to take this matter to the Middlesex County municipal court; there was nothing more that he could do. Calvin gave me an evil stare and said: "I want my stuff!" I responded calmly by saying: "All is fair in love and war. All I wanted was a little time." Calvin and the officer left my office building.

As soon as Calvin got to his office, which was within walking distance, he called me. "Why did you do that to me? Why did you take everything?" I responded by saying that I only took what belonged to me. I further explained, "I didn't want it to end this way, but you were unreasonable. I couldn't allow Jasmine to be without a place to live." Calvin begged me to see him. I didn't think it was a good idea. He suggested that we meet at a neutral location. "How about Fornos Restaurant on Ferry Street near Penn Station?" I said "Okay." My mother picked me up after work and Jasmine was in the car with her. I told her that I had agreed to meet Calvin at Fornos. She didn't think it was a good idea either. I told her that I thought I would be safe because it's a public place. When we pulled into the parking lot, we saw Calvin's car. I hopped out and told my mother to wait in the car. Calvin was standing near the entrance of the restaurant, so I saw him as soon as I walked in. We talked for a brief moment. All Calvin wanted to hear was that I was going to give him back the furniture. He didn't know where I had moved to so he also wanted to know where I was staying. I refused to share that information. I felt that he got exactly what he asked for. He said that I humiliated him. "Do you know how I felt when I walked into the apartment and everything was gone? I did a double take. I couldn't believe my eyes. When we met in my office that evening, I thought we agreed to work things out. Why did you do this Jackie?" I told him that I didn't really want to leave this way, but I didn't have a choice. "All I wanted was more time to find a place to live, but you refused. I did what I had to do."

We parted on what I thought was a civil note. I walked to the car and hopped in. My mother was behind the steering wheel. Jasmine sat in the middle of the back seat; she turned around, looked out the rear window, and began to laugh at Calvin who was in the car behind us. All of a sudden, out of nowhere, Calvin sped up, spun his car around us and positioned it in the middle of the street blocking traffic on both sides. He jumped out of his car and started yelling, "She stole my stuff! That lady in the car stole my stuff!" I couldn't believe what was happening. My mother told me to sit still, "Do not get out of the car." We made sure all the doors were locked, and our windows were rolled up. Then the next thing I knew police were on the scene. The police officer told Calvin he had to move his car. He was blocking traffic. He told the officer that I stole his stuff, so the officer approached my side of the car and motioned for us to pull over, which we did. Once

Calvin had parked his car, he and I got out of our cars. Calvin looked crazy and started yelling at the officer about his stuff. The police officer told him he was going to have to calm down, or he was going to arrest him for disorderly conduct. That got Calvin's attention. The officer asked for my side of the story, which I provided, in a calm manner. The Essex County police officer explained that the matter was out of his jurisdiction. He suggested that Calvin take it up with the Middlesex County court system, which is the same thing the other officer had told him earlier in the day. I was free to go. Calvin was pissed!

It took a few months, but eventually I started talking to Calvin again. Jasmine told me not to, but Calvin was persistent. He became the perfect gentleman again. We went on a few dates; he courted me hot and heavy. I started wearing the engagement ring again. Calvin was extremely apologetic, and I believed him. He wanted to get married and said that if we had a small wedding we could purchase a house. I agreed. We had a few marriage counseling sessions that didn't go well. The writing was on the wall that this was not going to be a marriage made in heaven, but, I ignored the signs. Nevertheless, we were married a few months later, on a Friday night. Calvin's father was his best man. A new friend of mine was my maid of honor. The only other people present were two friends of Calvin's, my mother Maxine, Jasmine, and my maid of honor's family. After the wedding ceremony, we went to a nice restaurant for dinner. From there, Carl and I went to Atlantic City for the weekend; Jasmine stayed with my mother Maxine.

We moved into a new house right away. Everything seemed new and wonderful until Calvin started to revert to his old ways. He started having bouts of depression. A few times, he balled himself up in a fetal position in the middle of the living room floor. He was rude and obnoxious and started staying out late at night. I worked hard to decorate the house; it was a beautiful three-story condominium with a two-car garage located in Newark. I wanted us to be happy, but Calvin was miserable. Jasmine liked her room and the fact that she had access to a swimming pool. She and her friends spent a lot of time at the pool that first summer we were there.

A few months into our marriage I missed my menstrual cycle. I was pregnant. My marriage was already shaky, and I couldn't imagine having children with Calvin. He was a mad man! When I told Calvin that I was pregnant, he wanted me to keep the baby. I told him that I didn't think it was a good idea because he wasn't happy in the relationship. Even though Calvin wanted me to keep the baby, he agreed to pay for an abortion. He didn't seem to be too upset about it until after the procedure was done. As we rode home in the car, he expressed his disappointment. And, I didn't care. All I knew was that Calvin had been exhibiting erratic behavior, and I didn't want to have his baby. From there things got progressively worse. In the midst of all the tension in my marriage, Jasmine continued to be the bright spot in my life. Calvin and I stayed married for one year.

Read on,
the story continues...

> "Teaching should be such that what is offered is perceived as a valuable gift and not as a hard duty."
>
> **~ Albert Einstein**

CHAPTER 10

The Groton Experience

Prior to my divorce, a wonderful thing happened that changed the trajectory of my life and Jasmine's. When Jasmine was eleven years old, someone told me about A Better Chance, a non-profit educational organization that helps minority students find suitable placement in some the best college preparatory schools in the United States. At the time, Jasmine was just starting 8th grade; she attended University High School in Newark. The school consisted of a middle school (7th and 8th grade) and a four-year high school (9th – 12th grades) for gifted scholars. The A Better Chance application was extensive, but I viewed it as an opportunity for Jasmine and me to become familiar with the application process for independent secondary schools as well as college. I provided the required documentation, mailed it and helped Jasmine prepare for the SSAT (Secondary Schools Admissions Test). Jasmine took the test twice; she took a pre-test and then about a month later she took the actual exam. All the schools we selected as schools of interest were located in New Jersey. I had hoped that Jasmine would be selected to attend a day school located not too far from home. But, none of the schools we selected extended an offer of admission to Jasmine. Instead, she received one offer from Groton School, located in Groton, Massachusetts -- one of the top ten best secondary independent schools in the country. Prior to receiving the letter of admission, I had never heard of Groton, Massachusetts or Groton School for that matter. The offer extended was for a full scholarship. Even though Groton is a boarding school located far from Newark, New Jersey, I felt compelled to check it out. Jasmine was invited to spend a weekend at the school to get a feel for the boarding school experience. I asked my mother Maxine to come along with us for the weekend stay, and she agreed.

It took us seven hours to drive to Groton from Newark on our first visit. When we arrived on "the circle," as the campus is called, we were quite impressed. The grounds were well maintained, the people were friendly and welcoming, and the environment was peaceful and serene. Jasmine slept in the dorm with the students; my mother and I rented a hotel room. During the day, Jasmine attended class with a student she was assigned to shadow while my mother and I toured the campus and attended informational sessions for parents of prospective students. It was a positive experience; but, Jasmine was only 12 years old (this was March 1997). Not only would Jasmine be far away from home but also she was required to repeat the 8th grade. That was a condition for admission. Neither was appealing to Jasmine.

During the drive home, I asked Jasmine how she felt about her experience at Groton School. She said, "It's nice and clean. I like it, but it's too far away from home." My mother Maxine absolutely loved the school, and I was trying to wrap my head around this amazing gift. Jasmine was offered a full scholarship, which included room and board, meals, transportation and a stipend. This was different from anything I had experienced. I didn't know anyone who had attended boarding school and certainly not that far away from home at such a young age.

When I told my grandmother "Mom" about it, she was adamantly opposed to the idea. She said, "Do not send my baby to Massachusetts with all those white folks." I responded by saying that bad things could happen right here in Newark among black folks. I talked to Jasmine long and hard about Groton. She didn't want to attend Groton because she didn't want to be away from her friends and family. I didn't want Jasmine to miss out on an opportunity of a lifetime. I encouraged her to try it out. I told her, "God would not have provided this opportunity if He wasn't going to make it possible for you to succeed. Just try Jasmine. I'm not sending you away to be unhappy, so if you don't like it, you can always come home. But I can't guarantee that another opportunity like this will come along again." Jasmine felt that I had made up my mind to send her to Groton, so she just prepared herself to leave home. That summer she spent a lot of time with her friends. As I previously mentioned, Calvin and I had bought a house in a new development in Newark. There were tennis courts and a nice size swimming pool on the grounds for homeowners and their friends to use. Jasmine and her friends thoroughly enjoyed the swimming pool.

The summer flew by. My marriage to Calvin was rocky from the start, so I focused my attention on Jasmine. I bought everything I thought she would need in preparation for her boarding school experience. Prior to Jasmine leaving home, we received an invitation to meet other Groton students and families in the New York area. The host family held the meeting in their home, which was located on Park Avenue in a penthouse. I will never forget the feeling I had as we stepped off the elevator into the penthouse. My stomach was in knots. I was so nervous, but I could feel the air of wealth – old money! I introduced Jasmine and myself; my mother was with us as well. I didn't have much to say. I simply took it all in. I listened intently and simply observed my surroundings. The house was decorated to perfection – beautiful artwork. The butler was attentive. The women talked about where to shop for the best bargains for school supplies. I must have looked sick because one of the women asked me if I was okay, "Do you want to sit down?" I did.

Jasmine and my mother did a better job of socializing than I did, although I did manage to exchange a few words with the ladies before we left to head home. I think I was rather quiet during our drive back to Newark. After dropping my mother off at her place, Jasmine and I went home. I remember going straight to my bedroom. I fell out on the floor – started praying and crying – crying and praying. "God please bless my decision to send Jasmine to Groton." Then suddenly it hit me. It was as if a small voice whispered – "If you're praying stop crying and if you're crying stop praying. It's going to be all right."

The day of Jasmine's departure came quickly. I prepared her as well as I could. My mother came along with us to help get Jasmine set up in her room. At a certain point on that first day at Groton, the Head Master called everyone to the dining room for lunch. I remember he asked me to sit next to him at the lunch table. I didn't eat or say very much. And then all of a sudden an announcement was made that all students had to leave with their big brother or sister (an upperclassmen who had been paired with the new second or third formers - 8th or 9th graders - to serve as a mentor). When the announcement was made, I froze. Tia Porter, Jasmine's big sister/mentor, rose from the table with Jasmine, and they left. I had to see Jasmine before I left the campus. I couldn't just let her go like that. Somehow I found Jasmine, and I kept hugging her tight. I started to cry – I didn't want to let her go. Jasmine was rather emotionless (later she told me that she had cried during the drive to Groton). I let her know how much I love her. My mother grabbed my arm and told me to let Jasmine go. I prayed, "Dear God, please bless my child." That was one of the toughest decisions I ever had to make. I knew that if it didn't work out, Jasmine would blame me for the rest of her life. I thank God for the courage to stretch out on faith and let the miracle happen.

During Jasmine's first year at Groton, Calvin and I divorced. I moved out of the house and stayed with my Aunt Rosetta in the second-floor apartment of her two-family house on South 16th Street in Newark until I was able to secure a new home. On June 30, 1998, I closed on a condominium within the same complex as my ex-husband. Jasmine was with me during the entire closing process. I borrowed $1,000 from my brother Joel, which I paid back in two weeks, but when it was all said and done, I had $8.62 to my name. From that point on, I worked two, sometimes three jobs to make ends meet. I had to furnish the condo – it was like starting over from scratch. The good news was that Jasmine and I had a place of our own.

My saving grace has always been my ability to be honest with my daughter. I have made some terrible mistakes in my life. But one thing I did right was to let my daughter know that I love her. I didn't just tell her; I showed her. I showed up for her. I sacrificed for her. I listened to her, and I valued her presence. My daughter gave me a reason to live and to strive for a better life. I felt I owed her a fighting chance.

Jasmine had numerous trials and triumphs during her five years at Groton, and so did I. While Jasmine was at Groton, I relapsed. I was still fighting internal battles. My feelings of inadequacy, insecurity, and anger had a grip on me. Even though I showed up at Groton to support her, I felt like people knew my story. I still very much wanted my mother Maxine to tell me the truth in her own words, which hadn't happened. Each time I got high, I prayed that God would remove drugs from my life. So much was at stake. I knew I had to get myself together, not just for myself but for Jasmine. I would get high on Friday or Saturday night (that same old pattern) and talk about the same old family stuff, but now I had feelings about my ex-husband to sort through as well.

One early morning after getting high, something came over me as I fell asleep. It was a dream that seemed perfectly real to me. Some force operated on me – cut my stomach open and cut away my desire to get high. I know it sounds crazy, but I swear that it happened. I continued to work hard, and I focused on my daughter. I stopped doing drugs.

For Jasmine's 16th birthday, I planned a big party. Sometime during the month of October 2001 my brother Scott called me. Scott was living in Newton, Georgia with Maxine and "Mom" at the time. Luckily, I was at my desk when he called. I thought he was calling to talk about the party, but I could tell by the sound of his voice that he was upset. "Can you talk?" he asked. "No, not really. I'm at work, and the area is rather open. I can listen, though. What's wrong?" "I'm just sick of this bullshit. Maxine and 'Mom' walk around like everything's okay but it's not. Maxine is always yelling at 'Mom' about something stupid like that's okay, and I'm sick of it because she won't talk about what really matters. Jac, I know you're my sister. I never told you, but I saw my birth records." I almost couldn't believe my ears. My brother was finally ready to deal with the truth!

Scott went on to explain that when he was working at UPS in Philadelphia back in 1989, he broke his toe and went to the emergency room at the University of Pennsylvania. When it was time to input his information, the nurse's assistant asked for his name, address, telephone number, date of birth and social security number. After inputting his information, the assistant asked if he had been to the hospital before. Scott answered "No." The assistant then said: "Well your name is coming up, look at this information is this you?" Scott said, "Yes." It turns out, Scott was born at that very hospital. He was able to see his birth records, which clearly showed that Maxine Hurtman is his mother. No information was provided in terms of who the father is. Until this moment, Scott had never shared any of this with me.

He said that he asked the assistant to print the information for him but for some reason he wasn't able to get a print-out, but now he knew without a doubt where he was born and who his mother really was. He went on to tell me that he called Maxine and "Mom" to tell them what happened but they acted indifferent. Sometime after he discovered the truth, he asked an aunt of ours, Aunt Pat, about it. Aunt Pat is really our cousin but since she grew up close to my mother Maxine (she's my mother's first cousin) we always referred to her as Aunt Pat. Scott told Aunt Pat that he saw his birth records and he knows that Maxine is his mother. Aunt Pat didn't say a word. Scott said it was as if she couldn't hear him. He was really upset by that, but he had kept it to himself until now. I could hear the pain in his voice; it was so familiar to me. I had been trying to get Scott to see the truth for years. He was finally fed up.

Scott told me that he wanted to leave Georgia. "I wish I could leave right now. I need to leave this house before I hurt somebody." I continued to listen to him share his feelings. When he had said all that he wanted to say, I suggested that he come to New Jersey or Philadelphia. I told him that I would ask Joel if he could stay with him for a while, which I did. I remember telling Scott, "Stretch out on faith and let the miracle happen." Within a few days, Scott left Georgia. He took "Mom's" pick-up truck and drove to Philly.

Jasmine's sweet sixteen birthday party was held on Saturday, November 24, 2000; her actual birthday was on the 25th. The party was well attended, and the special surprise was that her uncle Scott was present, whom Jasmine affectionately refers to as "Tio". Maxine and "Mom" didn't know that he was going to be there either. There was friction between them about the truck because "Mom" said that Scott took her truck. Maxine said that she had paid for the truck, so it was hers; she told Scott that he could take it. As a result, "Mom" was left without transportation of her own from that point on. Scott stayed at Joel's house and ended up working with Joel as a real estate agent for several years.

Quite a few of Jasmine's Groton friends who lived in the New York area came to her birthday party. Friends and family members came from far and wide; it was truly a time to remember. During the program, I read the following poem to Jasmine, which is an excerpt from a book given to me by my father, ironically entitled *The Secret of the Ages* by Robert Collier. Inside the front cover of the book he wrote: **"11/22/84 To Jackie From Daddy"** When I read the poem, I substituted the word "daughter" for "son" and word "mother" for "father."

A Father's Prayer

"Build me a son, O Lord, who will be strong enough to know when he is weak and brave enough to face himself when he is afraid; one who will be proud and unbending in honest defeat, and humble and gentle in victory.

Build me a son whose wishbone will not be where his backbone should be; a son who will know Thee – and that to know himself is the foundation stone of knowledge.

Lead him, I pray, not in the path of ease and comfort, but under the stress and spur of difficulties and challenge. Here let him learn to stand up in the storm; here let him learn compassion for those who fail.

Build me a son whose heart will be clear, whose goal will be high; a son who will master himself before he seeks to master other men; one who will learn to laugh, yet never forget how to weep; one who will reach into the future, yet never forget the past.

And after all these things are his, add, I pray, enough of a sense of humor so that he may always be serious, yet never take himself too seriously. Give him humility, so that he may always remember the simplicity of true greatness, the open mind of true wisdom, the meekness of true strength.

Then, I, his father will dare to whisper, 'I have not lived in vain.'"

--General Douglas MacArthur

Given that Joel, Scott and I were together in the presence of friends and family, there was underlying tension. I introduced Scott and Joel as my brothers but at that time, Maxine and "Mom" were still holding on to the story that Scott was "Mom's" son. That old lie still had its grip on our family.

After the party, Jasmine returned to school. She had begun to make a name for herself at Groton. She was applauded by a number of students and parents for being the first person of color on the Groton circle to extend herself time and time again to help new students of color get acclimated to the school.

The Groton experience was challenging for Jasmine and for me. But, ultimately we are better for having survived it. There were some rough moments – times when we didn't know how we would get through it. Not only did Jasmine get through it, but she also triumphed.

After graduating Groton, Jasmine went on to attend Hofstra University. By this time, I had returned to school and desperately wanted to complete my undergraduate studies before Jasmine got her college degree. Initially, I had hoped to obtain my college degree before Jasmine graduated high school but since that didn't happen, I strove to complete my degree requirements before Jasmine graduated college. I worked full-time during the day and went to school at night. In May 2005, I completed the course requirements for a Bachelor of Arts Degree from Thomas Edison State College. Jasmine graduated with honors the following year from Hofstra University.

Once Jasmine graduated Hofstra, she had one success after another. Seeing Jasmine thrive motivated me even more to succeed. After obtaining my undergraduate degree, I returned to school a few years later and in 2010, I graduated from Rutgers University with a Master's Degree in Management and Labor Relations. Jasmine went on to complete the Cosby Screenwriter's Fellowship at the University of Southern California and decided to make Los Angeles her home.

Jasmine and Scott—Groton School Prize Day

CHAPTER 11

How a Lie Became the Truth

Just recently I found out that my mother Maxine and my grandmother "Mom" sent money to my father John Hurtman on a regular basis. I know this is true because I've seen the canceled checks. The money was supposed to be used to buy clothes and food for Scott and me but instead my father used the money for his own purposes, mostly he gambled it away. Wasn't it apparent that the money was not being spent on us? How could they have been so fooled by this man? When they saw us, we always had old, worn out shoes and hand-me-down clothes that were in horrible condition.

My grandmother "Mom" has always acted like she was Scott's biological mother. She told everyone she came in contact with that Scott was her son. Since Scott was born in Philadelphia, none of the folks in the city where my grandmother lived (Reading, Pennsylvania), questioned her about it. Even if people thought that my grandmother wasn't Scott's biological mother, they accepted this. But didn't somebody see our mother Maxine during her pregnancy? Was she really that overweight that no one noticed her stomach grow? Was she kept so isolated from family and friends that no one knew that she was pregnant? Evidently, the answer is "yes" because no one ever challenged my grandmother "Mom" when she introduced herself as Scott's mother. What is still hard for me to understand is why my mother Maxine never announced to the world that she is Scott's biological mother. Instead, she perpetuated the lie by remaining silent.

My mother Maxine knows the truth, but she won't speak up. She must have been sworn to secrecy, to her own demise, and the only way the truth would have been told before now is if my mother would have told it. John Hurtman didn't tell it in his lifetime because if he did, then he would have to admit to being a pedophile, child molester, and a child abuser. He considered himself a pillar of the community, an intellectual, an entrepreneur, the quintessential businessman, husband, and friend. He wouldn't let the truth touch him with a ten-foot pole. And Nan, "Mom", my grandmother, was complicit. Her silence spoke volumes. By keeping quiet, she allowed the abuse of my mother Maxine to continue, which sent the message that she condoned what was happening. Responsible people clean up their messes. But when a mess is made that gets covered-up, the message sent is that the mess is acceptable. If there is an agreement to keep the mess a secret, then the few who know the truth must agree to tell a unanimous story - a lie. And, the story must be airtight. My mother Maxine never told a soul that Scott was her son. She was near him his entire life but always acted as if Scott was her brother. The truth was hidden in plain sight.

When Scott and I lived in Philadelphia, our father told everybody that we were brother and sister. It was alright to be brother and sister in Philadelphia because my mother Maxine and grandmother "Mom" weren't around. My father's wife at the time, Marty, played the role of our mother; no one in Philly had any idea who Maxine or "Mom" was. Some of our acquaintances did ask who our mother was, but we would simply tell everybody that Marty was our mother. As we got older and the questions became more piercing, I remember wanting to tell people that Marty wasn't my "real" mother but then, how could I explain that my "real" mother was not here with me? I didn't know why my mother Maxine had given me up, so I didn't want to talk about it with anybody.

The story wasn't challenged until I questioned it. As a child, I had to accept what my elders told me. But as I got older, I started to see people and situations for what they really are. I don't know who the mastermind behind this lie was, my father John Hurtman or my grandmother "Mom." I'm inclined to believe that it was my father because he was the initiator of the sexual abuse, so all the other lies that were told were by the enablers around him to cover up his transgressions.

How did the lie become the truth? The lie became the truth because no one questioned it or challenged. Everyone accepted it as the truth...except me. I challenged the lies. But, as a child, my elders ignored me and when I became an adult, they still stuck to their story despite my pleas. Just because my elders told me the lie and refused to tell the truth, it didn't change the truth. If you tell a lie long enough I guess in your mind it becomes the truth (or does it?). I always knew that Scott was my brother. I always knew that John Hurtman was my father. I also knew that Joel and I have the same father. I just didn't have proof. What adds to the drama of this story is that none of my father's children were actually raised by their biological mother. Even though my grandmother "Mom" took Scott from our mother when he was a baby, Marty raised us. I left Marty and my Dad when I was nine years old, and Scott left them when he was fifteen. My dad took Joel from Marty when he was four years old; Joanne raised him. Joel left Dad and Joanne when he was sixteen. It's such a convoluted charade.

I fought my entire life to find the truth, but it wasn't until January 2014 I finally got confirmation of that what I believed to be the truth. On February 3, 2014, my brothers, Scott and Joel, my mother Maxine and I had a DNA test done to prove paternity. The test results confirmed with 99.99 percent accuracy that Jon, Joel, and I have the same father, John Alexander Hurtman. The weight has been lifted, and the truth is documented. I was surprised that Maxine was willing to provide a blood sample for the DNA test, but I'm grateful that she did.

Ironically, my father shared the following poem with all his children (see next page):

If you want a thing bad enough

To go out and fight for it,

Work day and night for it,

Give up your time and your peace and your sleep for it,

If only desire of it

Makes you quite mad enough

Never to tire of it,

Makes you hold all other things tawdry

And cheap for it,

If life seems all empty and useless without it,

And all that you scheme and you dream is about it,

If gladly, you'll sweat for it,

Fret for it,

Plan for it,

Lose all your terror of God or man for it,

If you'll simply go after that thing that you want,

With all you capacity,

Strength and sagacity,

Faith, hope and confidence, stern pertinacity,

If neither cold poverty, famished and gaunt,

Nor sickness, nor pain of body or brain,

Can turn you away from the thing that you want

If dogged and grim you besiege and beset it,

You'll get it!

by Berton Braley

The behavior my father exhibited with women showed me the importance of an honest man. Although my father gave the appearance of a good man, in reality, he was a liar, a cheat and an abuser – a total fraud. He dressed up like a businessman and pretended to have it all together, but he wasn't successful at all. Publically, he acted like an accomplished intellectual but privately he was a tyrant, often times exploding with the slightest provocation. For the better part of his life, he didn't even have a job. He had women, though, who made him look good!

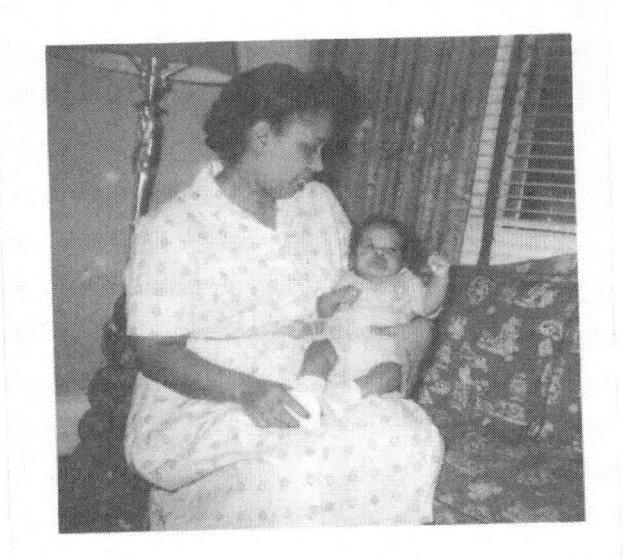

Our grandmother "Mom" holding my brother Scott.

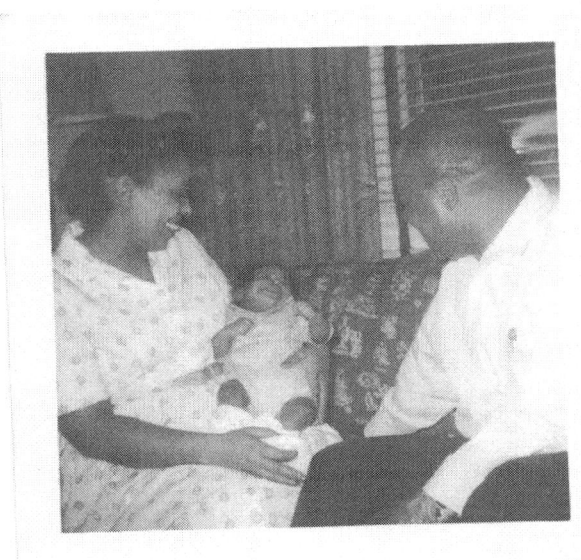

Our grandmother "Mom" with our father John Hurtman and my brother, Scott.

Our mother Maxine holding Scott. (Photo taken the same day as previous photos with our grandmother "Mom" and our father John Hurtman.)

> "You think your pain, and your heartbreak are unprecedented in the history of the world, but then you read. It was books that taught me that the things that tormented me most were the very things that connected me with all the people who were alive, or who had ever been alive."
>
> **~ James Baldwin**

CHAPTER 12

Reflection

"Atrocities happen every day, and you never
know what someone is dealing with behind closed
doors. So be kind." ~ Jackie Harden

I can't imagine how our mother Maxine felt growing up in an abusive household that was predicated on appearances. All I know is that she never announced publicly to anyone that Scott is her son. Even though she was around him most of his life, when our grandmother "Mom" introduced Scott as *her son,* Maxine never contradicted her. When I was born, Maxine and my father John Hurtman went so far as to falsely accuse a young man of being my father. As the story goes, John Hurtman had the young man incarcerated for non-payment of child support.

Evidently, everyone was in denial. There were layers upon layers of deception, and it took many years for me to get my brother Scott to face the truth. I understand his dilemma. As a child, our grandmother "Mom" was the only mother he knew; he always referred to Maxine as his sister. He accepted John Hurtman as his father because we always referred to him as Dad or Daddy. However, when he finally left Philadelphia and moved to Newark, I began to badger him about the fact that Maxine is not only my mother but his mother too. He didn't want to acknowledge Maxine as his mother because Maxine denied him, or, at least, it appeared that way.

At a certain point, I felt that everybody in my family resented me for not going along with the lies. I simply could not understand how or why people who claimed to love me would subject me to so much pain. I have often spoken of the hope that I saw in my daughter Jasmine's eyes that compelled me to want to do better. And, I don't understand why my mother Maxine didn't see hope in my eyes. Then I'm reminded that I'm the result of incest. I was never a child that she wanted; but, at least, she did acknowledge me as her daughter.

You might wonder if Scott and I ever confronted Maxine and "Mom" about all of this; yes, we did. A few years after Scott saw his birth records and realized that what I was telling him all along was true, he wanted to confront Maxine and "Mom." I agreed. For Mother's Day weekend in 2003, we decided to drive to Georgia to speak with them about our identity. We let Maxine know ahead of time that the purpose of our visit was to have a conversation with "Mom" and we wanted her to be present. Maxine was all for it, although she would never confront "Mom" on her own.

We drove straight through from Philadelphia to Newton, only stopping to get gas and to go to the bathroom. Needless to say, we were exhausted when we arrived in Newton, Georgia. "Mom" and Maxine were happy to see us. After resting for most of Saturday, on Sunday morning, Scott approached me and asked: "Are you ready?" I responded by saying "This was your idea, so I want you to take the lead." He said "Okay. Let's do it." Our grandmother "Mom" was sitting in the living room in her electric wheelchair, so I went to our mother Maxine, who was in her bedroom at the time, to tell her that we were ready to have the conversation. She immediately got up, and we all met in the living room.

Scott began the conversation by telling "Mom" there's something that we want to talk to you about. He went on to say, "I know that Max is my mother and John Hurtman is my father." "Mom" fired back "You are mine! I took you because Max didn't want you! She was going to give you up for adoption!" Maxine then said, "That's not true." "Mom" said, "Yes it is Maxine, and you know it." I jumped in to ask "Mom" if she knows who our father is. "Mom" quickly responded by saying, "As far as I know your father is some young man that your mother was dating back then." I retorted, "No, our father is John Hurtman." "Mom" said, "No he isn't. I don't know anything about that." I then said, "My mother told me that she told you a long time ago." My grandmother "Mom" cut me off and snapped, "No she didn't. She never told me that." Maxine said, "Yes, I did Mom!" Mom responded by saying "No, you didn't Maxine!" Scott jumped in and said, "Mom we just want the truth!" "Mom" started to cry and said, "I may as well die. I don't know what you're talking about. I did the best I could. Maxine didn't want either of you. She didn't take care of you – I did!"

"That's not what this is about 'Mom.' We want the truth!," I declared. At that point, "Mom" had a blank stare on her face. It was as if a stone wall had been erected inside her mind. All of a sudden the phone rang. Maxine checked caller ID, and it was my daughter, Jasmine. Maxine answered the phone, and everybody took turns talking to her. The purpose of the call was to wish Maxine, "Mom", and me "Happy Mother's Day." Once the call ended, we attempted to resume the conversation with "Mom," but she shut down. She didn't want to hear anything more we had to say so she grabbed her cane, got up from her wheelchair, and slowly walked down the hall to her bedroom. She then crawled into bed. Shortly thereafter, Scott and I decided that we were going to pack-up and hit the road. We had a long drive ahead of us. Before leaving, I went to see "Mom" to say good-bye and to tell her that I still love her. With tears in her eyes, she looked at me and said, "Well, I don't love you!" I couldn't believe my ears, but I just turned and walked away. I said good-bye to our mother Maxine and told her that I love her. Scott said his good-byes as well. We then got in the car; both of us were upset about what had just happened. There was silence for a good portion of the drive home.

What's remarkable about my family is that through all of the lies, chaos, and confusion, we remained close. I must admit that there were periods of time when I pulled away from our mother Maxine and our grandmother "Mom", but Maxine would eventually call me, and I would eventually start talking to her. And so it goes...

I had to learn to forgive everybody for everything including myself. There is some good in the worst of us and some bad in the best of us. We are all works in progress. However, when it comes to our children, we really do owe it to them to do better. Their life is a precious gift that we must cherish and protect.

Even though our grandmother "Mom" nurtured my brother Scott and me, I often wonder what happened in "Mom's" life that made it possible for her to treat **our mother Maxine** the way she did. I witnessed our grandmother make Maxine the brunt of her jokes. I saw our grandmother ridicule Maxine in the presence of other people as if she were a child; Maxine would simply laugh it off or walk away. She withstood the abuse her entire life. Now all I have is hope that **our mother Maxine** will have a conversation with us, her children, about her life. She has not spoken her truth.

Many years ago, I decided to write a book about my life. I intended to entitle the book *The Woman Next Door, The Little Girl Inside* because I distinctly remember that after being sexually abused I no longer wanted to go outside to play. I felt dirty. I felt different. Life got real serious – no more fun and games for me. Even though many years have passed since that fateful day when I was sexually molested for the very first time, I still remember how I felt. That little girl is still within me. To many, I may be the woman next door. No one would ever know my story if I didn't tell it. And, it's true for all of us... no one will ever know your story unless you tell it. After thinking it through, I decided to change the title of the book. However, I still wanted to use the original title I had in my heart for the book. So I wrote the following poem:

The Woman Next Door, The Little Girl Inside

You see me come and go

We've even exchanged pleasantries from time to time

You've watched my children play – haven't they grown?

I go to work every day and come home

I take care of my family

I show up at church on Sunday and attend prayer meetings on Wednesday

For all intents and purposes, I'm an ordinary woman

But there's a secret I've been keeping

    ~ a secret about who I am

Actually, it's a lie I was told

    ~ a lie I believed for far too long

That lie became the truth, so we pretended

    ~I played my part and so did you

But the little girl inside started to emerge

    ~she wanted to get real, to face what is true

You were there. You saw her asking questions ~~ seeking answers

What did you do? You stood silently ~~ said nothing

    ~then turned and walked away

You became a part of the lie, and that lie I will expose today

You see, that woman next door is far from ordinary

    ~she kept your secrets; she bore the pain

    ~the pain of abuse, abandonment, and lies

She may walk tall, speak kindly, seem refined and hold her head high

But underneath the polished exterior is a story

~a story that will blow your mind

Look ~~ there she is...

Show some compassion. Do not judge.

That woman next door... That little girl inside...

She could be YOU!

Dad and Joel

Joel and Scott

Jackie and Joel

Jackie and Scott

> "The goal is the same: life itself; and the price is the same; life itself."
>
> ~ *James Agee*

CHAPTER 13

The Grapevine

We are waiting on death... as I sit here May 9, 2015, watching my sick grandmother "Mom", I am reflecting on all the experiences we've had together. This is a very tough time for my family because we are witnessing the demise of the matriarch – Miss Nannie Mae, my grandmother, "Mom". This strong-willed, beautiful, resourceful, charismatic woman is fighting to stay alive. I can't help but wonder why she's fighting to live when the quality of her life has diminished... she's hooked up to an oxygen tank, she's got a catheter, and can't control her bowels. Her body is riddled with cancer; yet, her heart is still beating. She's calling out for people we don't see. She hears sounds that my family and I don't hear. So we sit and wait wondering if today is the day that my grandmother, the woman we all refer to as "Mom" will take her last breath.

When I think back over the years, I'm reminded of all the sins and sacrifices that I've seen "Mom" make. She's 93 years old now... but let's go back in time... I'm reflecting on some things I thought I'd never speak about. As I look at "Mom" in a weakened state, I can't help but remember...

But then, I hear "Mom" yell out, "Max! Max!"

I responded in a gentle tone, "What is it, "Mom"? What do you want?"

Mom quickly said, "I want Max! Call your mother!"

Just then my mother entered the room. "What is it "Mom"? What do you want?"

"Mom" then retorted, "My butt hurts!"

So my mother Maxine checked "Mom's" diaper and sure enough, "Mom" had shit on herself.

"Mom" passed on June 11, 2015 at 8:20 p.m. in Newton, Georgia. Maxine called me at 8:22 p.m. The week prior my mother Maxine called to tell me that "Mom" had only one week to live. I didn't want to believe it, but I had to accept it. "Mom's" quality of life had diminished significantly. She was confined to her bed. It was so hard to watch her body deteriorate. In her younger days, "Mom" was a force to be reckoned with. She had non-stop energy and could do almost anything she set her mind to accomplish.

My heart is saddened now because "Mom" is no longer with us in the flesh. However, I choose to believe that her spirit lives on inside me...

My "Mom" had the will to live. In her last days, she frequently said to me: "Everybody wants to get to heaven, but nobody wants to die. Until I know what's on the other side, I'll stay right here. I'm not giving up! If 'they' want me, 'they'll' have to come get me, 'cause I'm not going by myself!!!"

Also, it became clear that my mother Maxine kept "Mom" heavily sedated. As a result of her sedation, "Mom" did not want to eat. Consequently, "Mom's" body withered away right before our eyes. Admittedly, Maxine was tired. Heck, I experienced first-hand how tiring it was to attend to "Mom's" needs. She didn't have a consistent schedule. Many nights "Mom" would be wide awake. Not only would she stay awake all night but she would also stay awake for the better part of the following day. When she would become uncomfortable on one side or the other, she would request assistance to roll over to the other side. I give Maxine credit for caring for her mother at home until the very end. However, I know that "Mom" could have lived longer had she not been so heavily sedated and had she been properly nourished.

The last time I was with "Mom" was on Mother's Day weekend. On Mother's Day, my brother Scott was visiting "Mom" also. Sometime that morning, "Mom" called for all her children to come to her bedroom; we all stood around her bed: Maxine, Scott and me. "Mom" couldn't say much but at that moment, I could feel her love, pride, and joy for her children. We said "Happy Mother's Day!" I read the cards we had written for her. As I read to her, I held back my tears as best I could. Afterward, Scott and I asked "Mom" if she wanted to go outside, to see her beloved grapevine. She said, "Yes!" So, we helped her get out of bed. We didn't have to pick her up; she used her own strength -what little she had- to pull herself to the edge of the bed. I grabbed under her arm to help guide her body forward and then helped her to stand. I positioned the wheelchair by her bed so that once standing she only had to shift her hips to "plop down" in the wheelchair. We changed the oxygen tank from the electric one to the portable one. Scott grabbed the handles of the wheelchair and proceeded to push her wheelchair through the bedroom doors down the hallway, out the back door, and down the ramp. It was a bumpy ride from the house to the grapevine, but she didn't complain. It was a clear sunny day. Once we got close to the grapevine, my brother Scott suggested that we take a few pictures using my cell phone, which we did. "Mom" marveled at all the budding grapes; the vine was loaded. She said that she was going to make sure to enjoy her grapes this year. The grapes would be in full bloom in August – just three months away. We didn't stay outside long because "Mom" was tired and wanted to go back to bed. "Mom" died just one month from the day we took her to her grapevine.

> "Know from whence you came. If you know whence you came, there are absolutely no limitations to where you can go."
>
> **~ James Baldwin**

CHAPTER 14

The Truth

It has taken me a very long time to get to the place where I can talk about my life freely and openly. For me, it is important to speak the truth because I know how the lies nearly destroyed me. My first contemplation of suicide happened when I was seven or eight years old. The adults around me expected me to act prim and proper, but they were perpetrating a fraud. My father wove a masterful web of deception and convinced the women who loved him to believe every dreadful lie he told.

Why am I sharing this story? The answer is simple: To heal. Arriving at a place of peace alone isn't enough for me. You see, I really want my family to heal, and I want every reader who can identify with any aspect of my story to know that you are not alone. You, too, can heal. You can and will arrive at a place of peace if you work for it. And it has taken a lot of work to get here.

After experiencing my lowest moments, which happened in my late twenties, I began the process of facing the truth, accepting the truth, and speaking the truth. Through drug rehabilitation, I met a psychologist who was an angel sent by God. Dr. Angela Purelli helped me to see that it wasn't my fault that I was born into a chaotic mess. I did not create the circumstances into which I was born, but I had to take responsibility for my actions as an adult. As I said before, I will never forget the expression on Angela's face the first time I told her my story, my truth -- her eyes grew wide, and her jaw dropped, mouth wide open. She had asked me numerous questions before even she could wrap her head around what I shared with her.

Q: Your father is your grandfather?

A: Yes and No. My father married my grandmother "Mom" when my mother Maxine was very young (three years old – I think).

Q: Your father raised your mother? Your mother referred to him as her father, right?

A: Yes

Q: How old was your mother when your father started sexually abusing her?

A: I really don't know because my mother won't talk about it, but she was 19 years old when she gave birth to my brother and 22 when I was born.

Q: Where was your grandmother?

A: Good question – As far as I know, my mother, father and grandmother all lived in the same house together. My grandmother got pregnant by my father twice but miscarried both times. I hate to think that my father and grandmother used my mother to have children since my grandmother couldn't carry her babies full-term. I must tell you that my grandmother swears that she did not know that her husband was having sex with her daughter. She says that she believed that my mother had gotten pregnant by some boy she had been dating. That's what my father and mother told her and she believed them.

Angela helped me to come to terms with this ugly truth. There is no way to make this make sense because it will never make sense to me. The lies my father, mother, and grandmother have told me through the years will never make sense. I guess they didn't expect me to grow up. Maybe I wasn't supposed to live. Maybe I wasn't supposed to ask questions. Maybe I was supposed to perpetuate their lies. That's what my mother Maxine did. My mother chose to keep the secrets. My mother chose to remain silent. My mother chose to act like her stepfather is not my father. My mother chose to act like she didn't know that her husband had sexually abused me. She chose to write her husband's name on my birth certificate. She chose to act like "my abuser", her husband, is my biological father. She chose to change my last name. She chose to insist that I write "Jacquie Chavez" even though my name is "Jackie Hurtman." She chose to be a liar, just like her mother "Mom", and stepfather John Hurtman. That's the life she chose.

I made a decision to break the cycle. I made a decision to seek the truth. I made a decision to tell the truth. I made a decision to accept the truth. It has been a long journey to get here. Has it been easy? No. Has it been worth the fight? Absolutely YES!

I cried many tears. I attempted suicide several times. I endured self-inflicted pain. I tried to keep quiet and act the way I was told to act, but something deep in my spirit would not allow that to happen. And when I gave birth to Jasmine, that's when my transformation began. Jasmine became my reason to speak truth. Jasmine became my reason to fight lies. Jasmine became my reason to LIVE!

It's been interesting to observe life unfold. I remember asking questions about my family when I was a child and how family members would give me a blank stare as if I was crazy or invisible. However, as time moved on and the truth unraveled, now my family embraces me. I thank God for the spirit of forgiveness because this tragedy is almost unforgivable. There were days when I felt like killing everybody including myself. It's only by the grace of God that I'm still alive and able to share this story. It's only by the grace of a power bigger and greater than myself that I survived. It's only by the grace and mercy of God that I was able to forgive myself. The grace, the poise, and the love I exude are far beyond anything I could have created on my own. The Ultimate Power of the Universe must have known that I would tell my story – and give honor and praise where it is due. I could not have made it through on my own. I believe that I was commissioned to share this story – to give God the Glory!

I hope that every reader of this story will find the courage to be honest with him or herself. Every family has a story. Every family has challenges. I think my family's circumstances are extraordinary; but maybe by reading my story, it will help you to realize that you are not alone. You are not crazy. The life circumstances you were born into are not your fault.

We all go through something. We all have issues to overcome. Someone once said that we spend most of our adult life trying to overcome our childhood. The moment you decide to get real, tell the truth, and move forward, YOU WILL. Some of us have more to overcome than others but in the final analysis, it's all relative.

People, things, life circumstances are only as difficult to face as you make them. When you decide to live a life of honesty, integrity, peace, power and love, then that is exactly what you will experience. Be willing to do the work. Prepare to be challenged on every level and commit to doing whatever it takes to break the cycle of lies and abuse. We were created to experience an abundant life full of blessings and love.

Five generations - Granny, Mom, Maxine, Jackie, and Jasmine (sitting on Mom's lap)

On Wednesday, February 13, Martha N. Hurtman passed away at the age of 73, after a prolonged illness. Her passing was as she prayed for, calm and without pain. She married John Hurtman in 1967 and is survived by her son Joel Hurtman and her stepson Jon Hurtman and stepdaughter Jacquie Chavez.

Martha was born in Philadelphia in 1939, and grew up in Reading, Pennsylvania. She attended Mt. Holyoke College in Massachusetts studying Russian and French, and during the summer of 1960 served as a community volunteer in Bordeaux, France. She graduated from Mt. Holyoke in 1961 and became a volunteer community worker at the Albert Schweitzer Hospital in Haiti. In that role she learned Creole and worked with a female Haitian partner under the Haitian Department of Agriculture. She taught homemaking skills in rural areas of that country.

Returning to the United States in 1963, Martha became a teacher, first as a French tutor and substitute French teacher in the School District of Pottstown, Pennsylvania, then as a fifth grade school teacher in the same district. She taught Adult Basic Education for the Philadelphia Board of Education for five years then served as a Playgroup Teacher in Southwest Germantown. Along the way, she also worked successively as a typist, translator, bookkeeper and claims manager for the Philadelphia Art Institute, Music Data Company, Wissahickon Realty and the MC Metal Craft/Coast to Coast Health Care Corporation.

Martha dedicated herself to Jehovah by water baptism on May 16, 1975, and from September 1, 1987 she served as a Regular Pioneer Minister until her death teaching and praying with many whose first language was French or Haitian Creole. She was devoted to her God. While she was physically able, she spent her life in the ministry in the City, and during her retirement years worked closely with fellow residents of similar faith at the Phillip Murray House on Old York Road. At the moment of her death, Martha remained faithful and confident in the hope of life everlasting in a paradise earth.

About the Author:

Jackie Harden is an author, fitness instructor, and human resources professional residing in Newark, New Jersey. She shares her truth with the hope that it might inspire the reader to get in touch with theirs.

To find out more visit www.jackieharden.net.

As an independent author, word of mouth and personal sharing are critical to our success. If this story moved you, there are several ways that you can help share it:

1. Tell your friends and family members about the book. Pay it forward and give the book as a gift.

2. If you know of groups or organizations that could benefit from the book's message, please contact us via the website at www.jackieharden.net to schedule a speaking engagement.

3. If you're affiliated with a youth group, women's shelter, drug rehabilitation center, or any other support group in need of an encouraging word, please let us know. We would love to connect with you.

Thank you for your support.